C

'*Sense and Respond* is a radical departure for the entire service sector, a dramatic shift in thinking that could revolutionise services in the same way as Six-Sigma and TQM transformed the world of production. Congratulations on this brilliant contribution – we will all benefit immeasurably.' – **Roger Camrass**, *Director, Business Transformation Group, Fujitsu. Senior Associate, Judge Institute, Cambridge University. Co-author of 'Atomic: Reforming the Business Landscape into the New Structures of Tomorrow'*

'Inside the service industry is a growing revolution in the thinking behind the operational design and practice of serving customers. Striving towards "perfection-in-purpose", businesses can generate radical and effective change to deliver sustained business results. Lean service has now arrived.' – **David Clift**, *Chief Business Architect, Efficiency & Transformation, BT Wholesale Operations*

'Refreshing, practical, and a huge step forward in understanding customer-based business growth!' – **Derek Williams**, *Chief Executive, Society of Consumer Affairs Professionals (SOCAP) Europe and founder of the WOW! Awards*

'A fascinating and important extension of lean concepts into the realm of services.' – **Nick Oliver**, *Professor of Management Studies, Judge Institute of Management, University of Cambridge*

'In reality, this is a culture change on a massive scale in which learning is seen as central to business success. This approach transforms thinking behind the delivery of service, knowledge and innovation in organisations.' – **Dr Joel Cutcher-Gershenfeld**, *Senior Research Scientist, MIT Sloan School of Management, and Executive Director, MIT Engineering Systems Learning Center. Co-author of 'Valuable Disconnects in Organisational Learning Systems'*

'This book will provide managers with a set of new perspectives, which are critical for today's challenging business environment. Managers will learn how to leverage their intangible resources in order to continually innovate and differentiate – activities that are the essential drivers for a sustainable competitive advantage.' – **Bernard Marr**, *Research Fellow, Cranfield School of Management. Visiting Professor of Organisational Performance, University of Basilicata*

'In order to survive, nothing less than the engagement of the whole organisation with the process of understanding and responding to customers is required. The concepts outlined in *the journey to customer purpose* will enable leaders and managers to rethink their roles and to view employees and customers from a new perspective. Nothing less will do in a world where economic power and markets are constantly shifting.' – **Professor William Carney**, *Professor of International Marketing, Instituto de Empresa, Madrid. Formerly Visiting Assistant Professor at George Washington University, Washington, DC*

'The authors provide a pathway to creating highly responsive organisations. The practical application of this approach establishes highly skilled, highly autonomous employees capable of capturing customer intelligence and seeking new ways to create value.' – **Gary Fisher**, *MA, CIPD, Innovation Fellow, The Business Partnership Unit, Aston University*

Sense and Respond

The Journey to
Customer Purpose

Susan Barlow,

Stephen Parry

and

Mike Faulkner

palgrave
macmillan

First published in 2005 by
PALGRAVE MACMILLAN
Houndmills, Basingstoke, Hampshire RG21 6XS and
175 Fifth Avenue, New York, N.Y. 10010
Companies and representatives throughout the world.

PALGRAVE MACMILLAN is the global academic imprint of the Palgrave Macmillan division of St. Martin's Press, LLC and of Palgrave Macmillan Ltd. Macmillan® is a registered trademark in the United States, United Kingdom and other countries. Palgrave is a registered trademark in the European Union and other countries.

ISBN 13: 978–1–4039–4573–0
ISBN 10: 1–4039–4573–X

This book is printed on paper suitable for recycling and made from fully managed and sustained forest sources.

A catalogue record for this book is available from the British Library.

Library of Congress Cataloging-in-Publication Data

Barlow, Sue, 1972–
  Sense and respond : the journey to customer purpose / Sue Barlow, Stephen Parry, and Mike Faulkner.
    p. cm.
  Includes bibliographical references and index.
  ISBN 1–4039–4573–X
    1. Customer services—Management. 2. Customer relations—Management.
  3. Consumer satisfaction. I. Parry, Stephen. II. Faulkner, Mike. III. Title.
HF5415.5.B377 2005
658.8′12—dc22   2005046467

10 9 8 7 6 5 4 3 2 1
14 13 12 11 10 09 08 07 06 05

Printed and bound in Great Britain by
Creative Print & Design (Ebbw Vale), Wales.

To our contributors, family and friends and especially our partners, Rhonda, Jacqui and Rob for their endless support and understanding.

CONTENTS

Contents

LIST OF FIGURES AND TABLES

Figures

Tables

ACKNOWLEDGEMENTS

Authors' joint acknowledgements

We never underestimated what a journey in itself, writing this book would be. There are many people who have provided support and contributed in many ways. Primarily, however, we acknowledge all those people who have embarked on the Journey to Customer Purpose who have inspired us with their courage, tenacity and integrity.

We would like to thank our publishers, Palgrave Macmillan, and in particular, Stephen Rutt, Anna Van Boxel and our editor, Andrew Nash.

We thank our contributors, Joel Cutcher-Gershenfeld, Barnard Marr, William Carney and Dan Jones, for their support and encouragement and for acting as our sounding boards on so many occasions. A special 'thank you' to Gary Fisher, whose constant enthusiasm maintained our motivation.

We especially acknowledge a number of key people at Fujitsu who established a new way of working: Gwenda Connell, Beverly Evans, Mark Kell, Tsuneo Kato, Keiko Nakayama, Freddie Moh Chew Hon, Kenta Takiguchi, Noel Butcher, Natasha Shortland, Jonathan Witts, Mark Perkins, Peter Holmes, Linda Courtney, Philippa Whittington, Martin Provoost, Dick Smolenski, Pat Hogan, David Walton, Alan Furness, Paul Gardner, Mick Beadsley, Jeph Hamilton, Caroline Swain, Maria Lorenz, Geoff Holbrook, Rob Jones, Nicky Newton, Paul Watson, Chris Waldron, Declan Hamilton, Rob Denney, Des Lynch, Philip Duncan, Jan Clausen, Ann Visser, Roger Camrass, Roger Sandell, Chris Moorhead, Robert Lim, Neil Stoner, Matt Service, Paul Bresnahan.

We are particularly indebted to Jacqui and Rhonda, who have worked extremely hard in the background preparing and proof-reading our material.

Susan and Stephen especially acknowledge Landmark Education, an international training and development company, for the personal journey of transformation they experienced, which gave them the insight to create possibilities for others and to understand the nature of leadership required to transform organisations around the world.

Susan Barlow's acknowledgements

This book is the product of learning and inspiration from many experiences and people; in particular, from those who, while leading transformation, have demonstrated outstanding commitment and bravery in unlocking the potential of people. For the production of the book, I feel a deep sense of gratitude to my close friends and family, and especially to Rob who has given selfless support. My life has been enriched with their love, friendship and the strength of their contribution.

Stephen Parry's acknowledgements

New ideas never spring into being spontaneously, but are built on the ideas that went before. I would like to say 'thank you' to a number of people who guided me in the right direction while providing support and encouragement along the way: to Alan Furness, who saw a new vision for services in the new millennium; to John Seddon, who many years ago introduced me to the world of systems thinking; to Jim Womack and Dan Jones, who changed the course of my interest towards lean production; to my wife Rhonda, for her constant support and patience; and finally to my father and late mother, for their loving support and encouragement.

Mike Faulkner's acknowledgements

To list all of those who have helped and inspired me through the writing of this book would almost require another book altogether. Suffice to say that those involved have been told – a heartfelt 'thank you' to all of them. I must single out Jacqui, my partner (soon to be wife), who has been instrumental in driving me forward: she has been my support and critic throughout and I am indebted to her. Much of my inspiration has come from Nordstrom. I never tire of ordinary people doing extraordinary things. When I first heard of how Fujitsu were benefiting from implementing this 'stuff' I just knew I had to know more. I have a passion for all things 'customer' and knew instinctively that the Journey to Customer Purpose was a new paradigm: it has been great to see; it has been great to write; it has been great to witness the results. This new paradigm enables ordinary people to do extraordinary things on a global scale.

Copyright material

The authors and publisher wish to thank the following for permissions to use copyright materials: author's material from *Gower Handbook of Call Centre Management*, 2004, is printed with the permission of Gower Publishing Ltd, Gower House, Croft Road, Aldershot, Hants, GU11 3HR; material from *The Business Channel*, Programme 1290, 2004, is printed with the permission of Einstein Network, London; material from *Managing and Measuring for Value: The Case of Call Centre Performance*, 2004, is printed with the permission of Fujitsu Services Ltd, c/o Firefly Communications, London; the adaptation of material from *Systems Thinking, Managing Chaos and Complexity*, 1999, is printed with permission from Elsevier, Oxford.

Every effort has been made to acknowledge individuals and should we have inadvertently omitted anyone we sincerely apologise. We have also endeavoured to trace all copyright holders but if any have been inadvertently overlooked the publishers will be pleased to make the necessary arrangements at the first opportunity.

Dr Joel Cutcher-Gershenfeld
*Senior Research Scientist, MIT Sloan School of Management,
and Executive Director, MIT Engineering Systems Learning Center*

In reality, this is a culture change on a massive scale. It is a shift to a culture that can see the value in recognizing 'disconnects' with customers. It is a shift to a culture where frontline workers have the skills and motivation to conduct root-cause analysis. It is a shift to a culture in which learning is seen as central to business success, not just an add-on activity.

A number of leading organisations have been placing increased value on the learning from customer service operations. What sets apart the approach pioneered by the authors of this book is the fact that it is embedded in the work itself. This is not just a nice additional thing for people to do: it is at the *center* of the work. As a result, even some of the most routinized and hierarchical work – answering phones in a call center – has been transformed into a knowledge-driven work system.

This is not the only knowledge-driven work system of note. In manufacturing, the Lean Production systems at auto companies, aerospace companies, and others have produced astounding results through the nurturing and implementing of many thousands of improvement suggestions each year (in the leading facilities). In other sectors as well we find Lean Enterprise, Six Sigma, and other transformations that value knowledge as the engine driving continuous improvement. The authors' work at Fujitsu has been proclaimed 'the Toyota of service operations'. In the same way that Toyota fundamentally transformed our understanding of the flow and delivery 'on demand' of product, materials, and knowledge in manufacturing operations, this approach has transformed our understanding of the flow and delivery on demand of support, knowledge, and innovation in service operations.

The knowledge economy is much larger than the relative handful of expert jobs that are usually highlighted in the popular press. Virtually all types of jobs face the challenge of change in this new economy. Knowledge, skills and capability are at the core of the challenge. At issue is whether the change can happen in a way that is respectful of and even enthusiastic about the contributions of *all* workers. Taking such an approach makes good business sense. Indeed, anything less will not consistently deliver what customers want, when they want it, at the price they are willing to pay. Moreover, it is the right thing to do – for the workforce and for society.

PART I

Putting the customer first

CHAPTER 1

The Journey to Customer Purpose: optimising business effectiveness

Meeting the customer's needs

Over the past few years, we have seen opinion emanating from organisations around the world espousing that 'the customer is king'. However, the customer's role has taken on a significance that is beyond the capability of most organisations today. Customer demand has increased not only because of customers' own search for choice and diversity but also because of the need for support due to deficiencies of existing products and service. Organisations respond to this increased demand in a number of ways, commoditising their services to offer high-volume, low-cost alternatives where efficiency is driven, but often with a cost to service effectiveness. These organisations become caught in a downward cycle and in order to survive are faced with the reality of competing on price and searching for more volume. Most organisations faced with this position explore low-cost labour sources for customer support; however, the *origins* of customer demand have not dissipated, because they are caused by the service organisation itself or by the customer's desire for increased value. Whatever the solution, therefore, the problems of increased demand remain unless the sources of *preventable* demand are removed rather than institutionalised.

An alternative response by some organisations is to try to move up the customer value chain and to provide a higher-quality premium service which can be tailored to meet changing customer needs. Few organisations of today, however, have the operational structures, the measurement systems, the technology, the processes or the practice to continually lock on to ever-changing customer needs and to respond appropriately.

This book offers an *alternative* philosophy. It proposes that every self-respecting operational, functional, and senior manager sit up and take a long, hard look at his or her business. It takes apart typical management training methodologies and demonstrates that the business of doing business has evolved. It rips apart the traditional norms, and encourages every person in an organisation to question the reality perceived. It puts the *customer* at the centre of all resultant actions; and it creates an excellent *workforce* – a workforce capable of flexibility, and one that adds value to customers and to the organisation.

In the past, organisations have been founded on the premise that customers will stay loyal if the product or service is good enough. The reality, however, is that customers are intrinsically fickle – they will move to wherever they get the best service, as they perceive it. Recently, customers have been recognised as more 'sophisticated', a typical corporate response to customers actually being more *demanding*. And customers are more demanding because they have more options, more channels, and more power. They are no more sophisticated than before – they just have the ability to make a difference. Customer loyalty is an outmoded concept, attached to the services and products of mass production. Customer Value Principles go beyond that and challenge companies to become loyal to the customer by continually sensing and responding to changing customer needs. The responsibility for loyalty resides with the *organisation*, not the customer.

Organisations that grasp the fact that customers are their lifeblood are differentiating themselves by understanding customer purpose and striving for Customer Value Principles. Contained in this book are the elements that can make organisations react to customer needs more effectively. Customer Value Principles are simply applied to customer data, systems, work flow, measurements and committed leadership.

Simply delivering goods and services to the specification of the marketing and sales teams is no longer acceptable. Trying to *make the customer fit the sales proposition*, instead of *fitting what is sold to the customer's proposition*, only serves to shorten the life expectancy or effectiveness of the business.

The Journey to Customer Purpose: customer service at the heart of the organisation

The 'customer service' ethic is vital, but too often it is simply something added into the annual report – it is a necessary evil, a 'bolt-on' used only to restore lost value to the customer. Very few organisations have yet learned that the customer is no longer just a king – the customer is now a *deity*.

In the new business world, the deified customer wields true power. The customer is the arbiter between success and failure. But this benefits the business, too, because businesses that are capable of *sensing* and *responding* to customers' needs are able to make the customer a true and loyal advocate. The customer becomes a surrogate sales force; and the practitioners of service excellence become surrogate customers within their own organisation.

Whilst differentiation through service is still a vital addition to any business process, organisations that embark on the Journey to Customer Purpose acquire the ultimate tools to engender customer loyalty, customer retention, and employee satisfaction. And this is only the beginning.

Learning from the customer

When implemented, Customer Value Principles put the *customer* at the heart of the organisation, creating a culture that is driven by knowledge about customers and based on leadership and analysis. This philosophy is drawn from Lean Service, Transformational Leadership, and Systems Thinking.

This innovative customer-focused approach devalues the mass-production management theories that dominated the 20th century, the goal of which was to push products and services regardless of the real needs of the customer. Instead, our approach creates a pathway towards the creation of a *Customer Value Enterprise*®. What is unique about the new approach? Many traditional improvement tools and methods may be blunt and are often ineffective; in many cases they are also applied for the wrong reasons. However, these same tools and methods, when used in concert towards customer purpose, are transformed into razor-sharp instruments of change. Using these instruments in conjunction with customer intelligence data, and engaging frontline staff in their application, creates a powerful force for transformation. The 'Sense and Respond' approach is quite simply a new way to design, build and operate organisations, so that they evolve continuously in response to changing customer needs.

A Customer Value Enterprise® recognises that the true customer intelligence resides with the frontline staff – those who have direct contact with customers, who are frequently required to pacify and interact with those customers. By tapping into this intelligence, the organisation becomes capable of measuring service failures *as determined by the customer*, not by the organisation. A business can identify the origins of unnecessary costs created by waste and eliminate these, yielding exceptional benefits for customers and at the same time improving service levels far beyond expectations. By using this intelligence, a business can change the way that it treats its customers: it can become proactive in raising its service levels way above those of its rivals; and most importantly it can secure repeat business and extended contracts by fully understanding its customers' operational environment (Einstein Network, 2004).

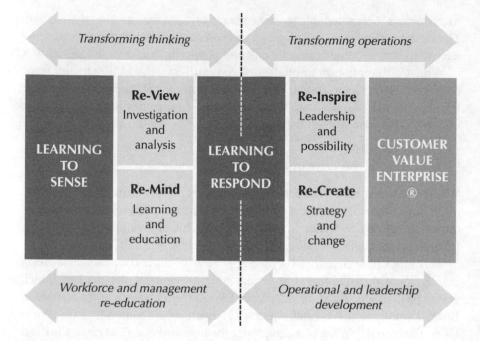

Figure 1.1 The Journey to Customer Purpose

By understanding and addressing the 'customer experience', a business that is sensing and responding (Figure 1.1) can offer world-class customer service in a very short space of time. The key to corporate success going forward is to create a *Customer Value Enterprise*® focused on customers. Yet while many organisations recognise this fact, very few are able to move fast enough because of their ingrained systems and processes. This approach can release these businesses from the shackles of standard practices.

In a Customer Value Enterprise®, the hierarchy is essentially turned upside-down. The role of the manager is changed from one of authority to one of support. The manager's central responsibility is to provide the necessary knowledge and tools to allow frontline staff to handle the needs of the customer and to assume responsibility for the end-to-end service. Frontline staff embrace this innovative culture. As they are the true experts, they assume the responsibilities of designing their own job roles, articulating to the organisation the needs of the customer, and identifying the knowledge and tools necessary to achieve customer success. This strategy uses human intelligence and human relationship-building skills as the starting point for organisational transformation. As relationships shift between staff, managers and customers, and as staff embrace new responsibilities, old assumptions and mindsets will inevitably be challenged – and to good effect. A Customer Value Enterprise® offers a new paradigm: an approach that breaks with the past to create breakthrough services.

Transforming your business

For an organisation to understand how it creates value for its customers, it needs to embark on a four-phase transformation journey (Figure 1.2).

- **Re-View**. Sense what matters to your customers, and measure the end-to-end organisational response capability.

- **Re-Mind**. Introduce *Customer Value Principles* to begin the process of influencing management thinking on the organisation and control of work.

- **Re-Inspire**. Provide Transformational Leadership coaching in the art of change to create possibilities and to break through to higher levels of organisational and personal performance.

- **Re-Create**. Start to build the operational structures that continually sense what matters and respond appropriately. Lay down the foundations of a Customer Value Enterprise®.

Customers are increasingly faced with a combination of automated telephone systems, technology, and personal contact. Whilst the telephony and technology are almost always of a consistent standard, the quality of personal contact is often diminished by out-of-date management systems that have evolved in different circumstances and now make it harder for staff to provide a genuinely customer-focused service. As customers are moved up the value chain, *customer satisfaction* should become the bare minimum, and *customer success and purpose* should become the Holy Grail. Businesses can achieve this by understanding customer purpose and then moving from the mass-production principles of yesterday to the Customer Value Principles of tomorrow.

Customer success can be realised by implementing the values of a new, customer-centric operational approach that has been tried and tested across various vertical sectors. By sensing and responding to customer needs, businesses can benefit from improved customer and employee loyalty. Organisations become both more innovative and more capable of responding and adapting to changing customer demands. The process requires no new technologies: it simply uses existing technologies to better effect.

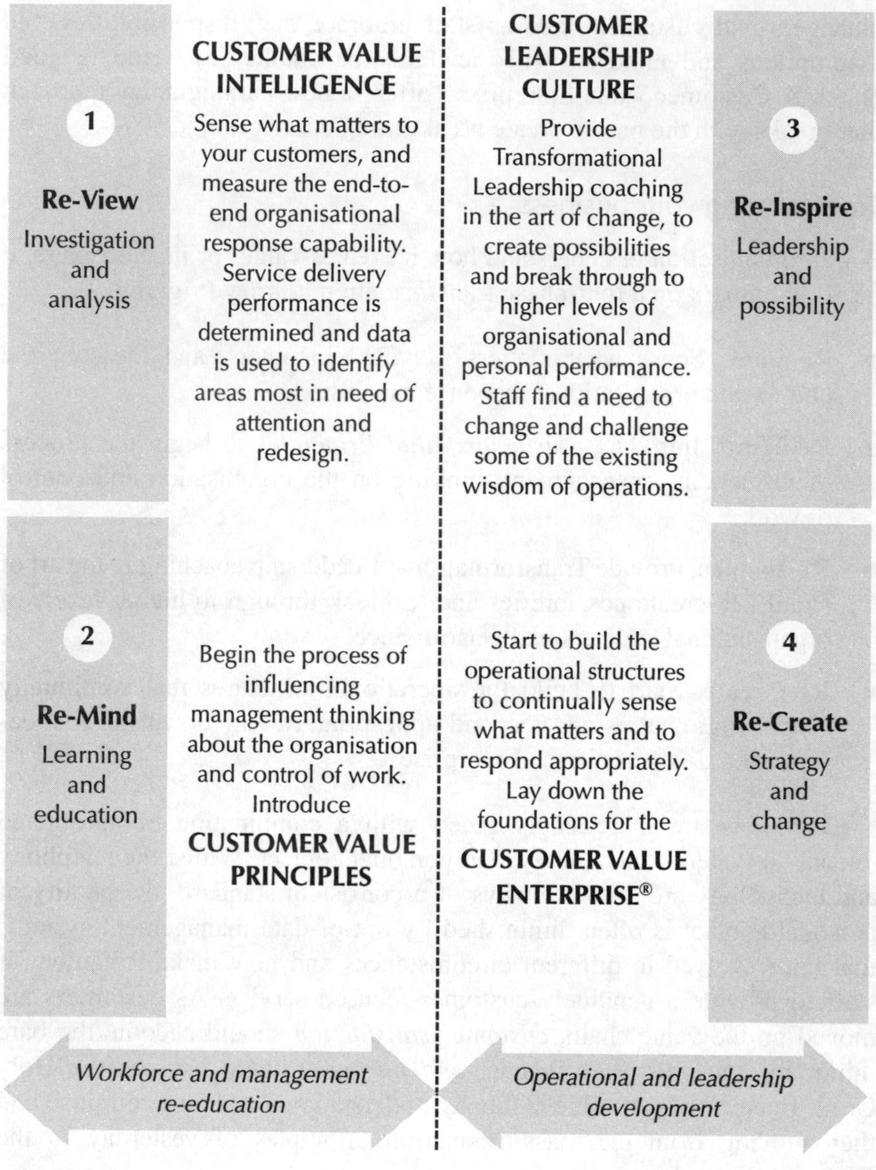

	CUSTOMER VALUE INTELLIGENCE	CUSTOMER LEADERSHIP CULTURE	
1 **Re-View** Investigation and analysis	Sense what matters to your customers, and measure the end-to-end organisational response capability. Service delivery performance is determined and data is used to identify areas most in need of attention and redesign.	Provide Transformational Leadership coaching in the art of change, to create possibilities and break through to higher levels of organisational and personal performance. Staff find a need to change and challenge some of the existing wisdom of operations.	**3** **Re-Inspire** Leadership and possibility
2 **Re-Mind** Learning and education	Begin the process of influencing management thinking about the organisation and control of work. Introduce **CUSTOMER VALUE PRINCIPLES**	Start to build the operational structures to continually sense what matters and to respond appropriately. Lay down the foundations for the **CUSTOMER VALUE ENTERPRISE®**	**4** **Re-Create** Strategy and change
	Workforce and management re-education	*Operational and leadership development*	

Figure 1.2 The four-phased approach

Six business imperatives

The journey from mass production to Customer Value Principles may be seen by some employees and managers as going a step too far or providing a challenge too great. Once the thought processes of staff have been transformed, however, and once this new way of thinking has been implemented via a step-change process, customer success will be accomplished in a revolutionary and quantifiable way. The advantages soon become self-evident to the staff too, and they experience greater job satisfaction.

Research, experience and general consensus present six primary business imperatives which are accepted across the majority of organisations throughout the world. These business imperatives apply to *all* industry sectors, irrespective of the organisational size or location:

- Optimise costs.
- Improve customer satisfaction.
- Create innovation.
- Increase employee satisfaction.
- Create differentiation.
- Improve profitability.

The adoption of Customer Value Principles will create uplift and positive organisational outcomes in relation to every one of these imperatives. By thoroughly engaging employees in a non-traditional way, and by undertaking a transformational process that includes leadership, a business will achieve measurable results and will prosper. However, there is no generic rule as to how quickly the Customer Value Enterprise® will pay dividends – much depends on how well an organisation is already aligned to deal with customer demand. Committed adoption of Customer Value Principles will start to demonstrate results in months, not years. Institutionalising the principles into the corporate infrastructure will take longer. Exactly how much longer will depend on many factors. The organisation must first evaluate how it can currently sense what matters to customers, and then understand how it can respond end-to-end: only then can a clear picture emerge as to the scale and duration of the transformation activity.

Mass production vs. Customer Value Principles

There is a cataclysmic difference between mass production and the creation of a Customer Value Enterprise® through the application of Customer Value Principles (Figure 1.3). Customer Value Principles come from many sources – particularly from Lean Service and Systems Thinking – but the line between mass production and the Customer Value Enterprise® is not a continuum: these are completely different ways of working. You are either doing one *or* you are doing the other – you will not find yourself doing some elements of each.

Work to forecast	vs.	Work on demand
Process all demand	vs.	Remove unwanted demand
Batch and queue	vs.	Continuous flow
Prioritising and expediting	vs.	On-demand capability
Continuous improvement	vs.	Continuous value creation
Root-cause analysis	vs.	Root-cost analysis
Work to standard	vs.	Work through standards
Measure outputs	vs.	Measure capability of means
Deliver to specification	vs.	Deliver to purpose
People performance	vs.	System performance

Figure 1.3 Mass production vs. Customer Value Principles

Working to forecast vs. working on demand

Compare the activities and behaviours you would find in a mass-production environment with those found in a Customer Value Enterprise®. In the mass-production environment, the primary concern is to maximise all assets and capabilities. If there are several assets and capabilities, it is assumed that none of these should be idle: keeping them working all the time thus becomes the *driver* – the consideration that determines management actions (Womack and Jones, 1996).

Maximising production does *seem* to make logical sense – but only if there is demand for the product. If not, the business needs to reduce production. In the Customer Value Enterprise® world, however, the business aims to produce only in response to *known demand*; it doesn't build up inventories. You don't make things 'just in case', because if you did you might make the *wrong* things and waste resources, and you would certainly increase the cost of storage. Mass-production enterprises in the West are often driven by the production forecast: output is generated in the expectation that all products will be consumed. Many production companies are now moving to 'build to order' – that is, 'on demand'. The principles of operation between these two approaches are very different. In the 'on demand' world it is logical to keep some assets idle and to accept idle costs in exchange for the reductions in inventory, in storage costs, and in losses from discounting over-produced products. In the 'on demand' world, even the idle-time cost can also be recovered if the organisation uses this time to improve and optimise the value chain and thus to reduce the cost of production still further and to increase quality.

The term 'on demand' is used by many today to mean simply the transfer of transactions and ordering to the internet. While in many cases this is an effective means of providing customers with access to products, it does not necessarily mean that the end-to-end organisation has been set up to respond 'on demand'. Throughout this book we will not use 'on demand' to refer to an electronic shop window: rather we will use the term to signify *a complete change in how the organisation is designed, built and operated end-to-end*.

Processing all demand vs. removing unwanted demand

Whereas mass-production systems tend to process all demand and services irrespective of the nature of work, the Customer Value Enterprise® aims to *remove certain types of demand* – the demand that adds cost without adding value. The driver here is not just to do work as fast as possible, but actually to *reduce work* by *removing non-value added activities*. The thinking is thus very different.

Batch-and-queue vs. continuous flow

The way that work flows through an organisation is usually what is called *batch-and-queue*. Because of functional specialisation, the work gets fragmented. A given piece of work stops and starts each time it is put it into someone else's inbox or passed to another department: while waiting for someone else to get round to it, the work stays idle. The customer may also experience the effects of this when trying to track progress as the work is passed around departments – this too adds more work, creates no value, and increases frustration. Customers may feel as if they are being 'timeshared' by various people and departments.

In a Customer Value Enterprise®, the aim is to create continuous flow and to make sure that this flow is as short as possible. When you get any sort of service demand, you act upon it now, this moment. And you see the work through to completion – you don't half do it, put it in a queue and come back to it later (Womack and Jones, 1996).

Prioritising and expediting vs. on-demand capability

In the mass-production world, limited capability means that the business must choose to prioritise or expedite some things, and other things therefore have to wait. But waiting causes waste. In mass-production, managers think that they must prioritise and expedite because they do not have sufficient resources: yet the systematic prioritisation of work actually creates more work.

Prioritisation is a symptom of the disease it purports to cure. When instead you create *continuous flow* and *work on demand*, you remove this need to prioritise and expedite.

Continuous improvement vs. continuous value creation

In the mass-production world 'continuous improvement' is a familiar mantra. This aspiration has been around since the Industrial Revolution and has been the biggest message in the quality movement. And it is an effective aspiration – as long as the products or services remain fairly constant and predictable, without variety being demanded.

Continuous improvement towards perfection is not enough, however – what is needed also is *continuous value creation*. There is little point in producing something that has no defects if it doesn't completely meet the customer's needs. At the heart of a responsive business strategy, therefore, is a commitment to understanding what value looks like to the customer, and then to using the pursuit of continuous value creation as the driver for the business.

Root-cause analysis vs. root-cost analysis

In the mass-production world, attention is often focused on analysing the root cause of any problems that arise. Despite this analysis, however, action to cure the problem does not always follow. Why not?

To make change happen, the business also needs to focus on the costs of not correcting problems – the cost to the organisation, the cost to the customer (especially crucial), and the cost to society. Taken together, these costs provide the business case for change. In the Customer Value Enterprise®, therefore, change occurs when customer intelligence data has allowed the true origins of cost to be determined and quantified. In other words, *root-cause analysis* is superseded by *root-cost analysis*.

Working to standard vs. working beyond standards

In a mass-production world, the drive is to obtain standardisation. This makes sense provided that there is little complexity and variety in the nature of the demand, and that the adoption of 'standards' does not prevent improvement.

Having standard processes and standard products can help to ensure high quality, for example in manufacturing, but it can also lead to a work ethic in which 'working to a standard' (Seddon, 1992) is accompanied by the abdication of any improvement responsibility to the *owners* of that standard. This mindset, we believe, is the biggest constraint on creativity, innovation and workplace ownership. We are advocating instead a world in which employees work *beyond* standards, breaking through to higher performance and continually raising the bar.

Measuring output vs. measuring capability of means

In the mass-production world, the performance of individuals and departments can be measured by determining their *output* – how many items they have produced, how many they have sold, or how many they have shipped. Much more important to know, however, is what those individuals and departments are *capable* of doing: do they have the means of production overall, and what is the capability of the operation? It is actually much more productive for managers to spend time in developing the capability of their organisation than in trying to push the organisation to meet production targets. Whereas in the mass-production world you measure the performance of people and departments in terms of their output, in the Customer Value Enterprise® you measure performance in terms of the capability of means.

Capability of means is more important than *output*. For example, if you were asked to drive 50 miles when your car had only one gallon of fuel and a capability of 30 miles to the gallon, it would be silly to set out on the journey. The ability to measure capability can thus be more important than the ability to measure output.

In their book *Profit Beyond Measure* (2001), H. Thomas Johnson and Anders Bröms write encouragingly about companies that have moved away from 'managing by results' and towards 'managing by means'. They call upon managers to move from *targets* to *pathways*.

Delivering to specification vs. delivering to purpose

In the mass-production world, the business delivers to a contract or to specification and endeavours not to deviate from that. In the Customer Value

Enterprise®, continuous value creation accepts that customer purpose is constantly changing and that contracts can't keep up: instead of delivering what was *specified*, you need to deliver what *matters*. Construct your whole proposition to the marketplace around continuous value creation, and continually change your products and services to meet that proposition.

Traditional contracts and specifications can never keep up with changing customer needs. Although specifications may still be helpful in manufacturing, they will tend to constrain the delivery of services. Instead of working to a specification or contract and defining itself by *the products or services it delivers*, it is better for a service organisation to define itself in terms of *the value it creates*. This basis leaves the organisation free to experiment and to innovate with new products and services.

Flexible specialisation in a mass-production world is just a more sophisticated means of controlling customers. It is not about being flexible by offering variety, as in mass-customisation and personalisation: it is about responding quickly to customer purpose. In the mass-customisation world, the organisation is still in control; in the Customer Value Enterprise®, the customer is in control.

People performance vs. system performance

When things go wrong in an organisation, managers in the mass-production arena usually start to criticise their staff: 'You didn't make your quotas' or 'You didn't make your output numbers'. Yet performance problems can have other causes, such as when demand exceeds the end-to-end capability; when an unknown and inappropriate demand enters the system; or when someone along the value chain improves performance locally and inadvertently creates a knock-on effect downstream.

Factors such as these account for over 90 per cent of the variation in service performance (Edwards Deming, 1982). Most of this variation is outside the power of the individual – individual performance can only contribute as much as the constraints of the current system will allow. Performance is created by the system, not by individuals, so systemic changes are needed if there are to be breakthrough improvements. In the Customer Value Enterprise® model, changing the system is the responsibility of those who work in that system.

As has been said above, the mass-production paradigm contrasts significantly with the Customer Value Enterprise® paradigm, and there is no continuum from one to the other. Yet in practice most organisations currently work using mass production. How can one flip from one paradigm to the other? To make this shift takes strong leadership that allows staff to work in *both* ways for a short space of time while transitioning from one to the other. With a lot of courage, tenacity, honesty and clarity of purpose, staff and managers can drive the organisation from one paradigm to the other. This allows staff to experience both paradigms – and the flip, when it happens, is very quick.

Three major components are necessary. First, you need to *collect data about how your organisation responds to the real needs* – as opposed to the perceived needs – of your customers. Second, you need to *assess how your organisation performs end-to-end in achieving the customer purpose*. Once staff have collected the data, they can discuss it with their manager and talk more easily about change. Third, as well as gathering data, staff also need to *understand what the reality is like*. As they grasp this reality, they become better able to collect the data. This process thus becomes an iterative one with these three elements.

The type of change that we are advocating depends on learning the principles of all three and bringing all three together. Because they are so interdependent, change will occur only when all three are addressed at the same time.

The soft stuff is the hard stuff – and it's the *only* stuff

Encouraging staff to see the organisation as a whole

Lean, Six Sigma, Total Quality Management (TQM) and other management tools and techniques have contributed greatly to leaner working. Yet none of these has explicitly addressed the underlying change in thinking and behaviour that actually releases the potential of the people within the organisation. What we are arguing is this: *release the potential of your employees, and the employees will release the potential of the organisation*. If you don't address the fundamental thinking and behaviours of staff, programmes of change will be ineffectual – you may plough millions of pounds into making changes, consuming resources, time and effort, but unless you also change your employees' thinking and behaviours, you will probably have to do this all over again in a few years' time.

From the total organisation, select strategic points across the business. From each of those points, bring staff together with a cross-section of other staff – frontline staff, middle managers and first-line managers. Staff will have been working in an environment in which mass-production principles have been predominant (Gharajedaghi, 1999). Staff need to be taken through a reorientation process in which they are taught a different set of principles on which to design, build and operate an organisation – the lean principles of a Customer Value Enterprise®.

For the majority of people who come together in this way, it is a revelation to learn that there are different ways of running organisations – many will have been used to thinking that there is only *one* way. As they begin to consider it with more freedom, they will start to understand what their organisation really looks like and to see the organisation from the customer's perspective.

As the employees' awareness grows, reorientation can also provide the methods and tools that will help them investigate the organisation from the *outside-in* perspective instead of from the *inside-out* perspective. This new perspective will yield different data – data from the customer's perspective that actually tells you how the organisation appears to the customer to be performing end-to-end.

Encouraging staff to promote change

The reorientation process gives this group of employees a new awareness, and it gives them new tools with which they can investigate. But it also gives them the skill set to be Transformational Leaders within the organisation. From these meetings, employees go back to their workplaces and start to transform the organisation. And in the process they also start to transform their colleagues.

What staff need to do is to provide customer data and insight to their managers – and then let them be instruments of change. The managers' work is predominantly aimed at creating leaders who have a new set of principles, who begin to use new techniques of analysis, and who have conversations with the managers about the customer intelligence data they gather. It is staff themselves who will start to dismantle the structures of the old process and will change into a new mode of working; and it is the same teams that will then go further and create action plans to promote even more change.

Encouraging staff to talk with each other

It is not always easy to liberate staff in this way, however. A major issue is that many of these people will not be used to working outside of their own immediate work environment – they won't be used to looking at the organisation end-to-end, and they may wonder what is meant by 'end-to-end performance data'. Do they feel capable of talking to people in other parts of the business? Can they overcome their natural reticence and fear of the existing hierarchy?

To overcome these difficulties, we use Transformational Leadership techniques based on cognitive behaviour principles. These help people to take a thorough look at their own behaviour – how they can influence people, and how they can have non-threatening conversations with others that can lead to meaningful change. It is vital that such conversations be threatening neither to the organisation nor to the person who expresses challenging observations or opinions: managers will not get honest feedback if their staff feel that their careers may be at risk.

Conversations at all levels

The period of reorientation and fostering leadership is thus crucial to the start of the transformation. By the time they go back to their workplaces, these staff must know the theory, have already begun to analyse what the organisation looks like from customers' perspectives, have some real data to support the customer findings, and have learnt skills of conversation that will help them lead people at their level in the organisation. From that point they can begin systematically to transform the organisation. They can begin to create a *Customer Leadership Culture* in which leadership is demonstrated at all levels, particularly at the frontline, creating a culture in which customer needs are understood and acted upon on a daily basis. This begins to lay down the foundations for the Customer Value Enterprise®. By creating an excellent workforce, the organisation's management is releasing the full potential of the organisation.

Managing by letting go

Managers and their staff may both expect the managers to exercise command and control over all aspects of the business – especially if that has been the dominant style in the organisation (Seddon, 1992). Initially, if so, managers may need to dictate the drive to a Customer Value Enterprise®. However, the real aim of the programme is to deconstruct dictatorial management and to create instead an organisation in which all operational units take control of operations; in which customer intelligence data is gathered at the frontline by frontline staff; and in which this data is used to shape, in a customer-relevant way, *all* value-creating activities.

As the process takes hold, customer-facing operations start to focus on what matters to the customer. As they understand this, they start to innovate: they start expressing to the larger organisation the *needs* of the customers, and the *capabilities* that the organisation will itself require in order to meet these customer needs. Frontline operations will gradually put in place the systems, processes, technologies, reporting and value propositions that will do that. Working in conjunction with colleagues, they will join up all the disparate functions within the organisation, coming together around the common set of customer intelligence data.

This is a big responsibility, but customer-facing operations need to step up to it. Initially it may be hard to persuade them to do so, but if staff are encouraged and supported and if their experience and insights are treated with respect, they will begin to see that their ideas are being taken seriously and that they are having a positive impact on the functioning of their organisation. In many cases they will be correcting problems that they, if not their managers, have been aware of for some time. As change gathers pace, employees are likely to feel increased job satisfaction and a growing commitment to the process.

CHAPTER 2

Focusing on the customer:
a paradigm shift

'Old world' and 'new world' thinking

There is a well-known story about a traveller who came upon three individuals working with stone.

> Curious as to what the workers were doing, the traveller approached the first worker and asked, 'What are you doing with these stones?'
>
> Without hesitation the worker quickly responded, 'I am a stonecutter and I am cutting stones.'
>
> Not satisfied with this answer, the traveller approached the second worker and asked, 'What are you doing with these stones?'
>
> The second worker paused for a moment and then explained, 'I am a stonecutter and I am trying to make enough money to support my family.'
>
> Having two different answers to the same question, the traveller made his way to the third worker. The would-be philosopher asked the third worker, 'What are you doing with these stones?'
>
> The third worker stopped what he was doing, bringing his chisel to his side. Deep in thought, the worker slowly gazed toward the traveller and shared, 'I am a stonecutter and I am building a cathedral!'
>
> Source unknown

This story is often used to illustrate the need for purpose and meaning in the world of work – the need to be able to see the grand design and to feel part of something larger. As a metaphor for life, it works well; as a metaphor for work today, however, it raises some fundamental issues.

1   The type of the work done by the three stonecutters is the same: only their attitudes towards their work are different. The attitude of the third may seem especially admirable, but is it anything more than a psychological ideal which makes the worker feel better about his lot in life?

2   Does even the third worker really understand how his contribution systematically connects with the contributions of others? Or does he know only that someone else will integrate his output into the whole end-to-end process?

3   Does the third worker's attitude to his work also provide him with insight into how he may improve his work and gain insight into customer needs?

The story is set in a time when it took centuries to build a cathedral. The worker's job was probably handed down the generations in much the same way.

The higher purpose in the story was to create cathedrals in homage to the glory of God and as a reminder to the populace of the infinite splendour and majesty of the Creator – to be places of awe. One might suggest that the churchgoer is going to the cathedral because of its design as a place of worship simply because 'one size fits all'.

The work of the master craftsmen and apprentices could be insecure, dangerous and poorly remunerated, hence their banding together in guilds. The hierarchy and organisation of work served the purposes of creating higher meaning for the workforce and maintaining strict skill specialisation in an age when everyone was expected to know and keep their place.

Today's consumers do not behave in the same way as those earlier worshippers. Consumers are no longer content with 'one size fits all'. They have learned to demand individuality, customisation and personal attention – and they won't wait long for it! In addition, consumers are workers themselves and demand individual attention and personal growth in all aspects of their lives.

How can one create meaningful and productive work for staff to serve the diverse needs of consumers? Imagine a world in which the worker was not only the stonecutter, but also the architect and the builder – *and* someone who paid close attention to individual customers' needs! Clearly the structures and principles for designing and organising work would need to be fundamentally changed.

Many organisations, however, are far from flexible enough to cater for individual customers' needs. Their infrastructures and systems are set up like those used to produce the cathedrals of old, in keeping with an earlier way of working – a way of working that once helped them to serve their customers, but now hampers them in doing so.

The journey to a Customer Value Enterprise® is neither as difficult nor as hazardous as the process of building a cathedral. If you think about it, working within the mass-production environment is often very difficult and complex due to the desire to make accurate forecasts, to maintain maximum employee activity, and to try to standardise and plan in a world where customer demands and market drivers are creating discontinuous change. Detailed planning in such an environment is no longer feasible. Trying to maintain a model that has reached the end of its useful life just creates more complexity, frustration and loss of business. In contrast, what we are asking, quite simply, is that organisations understand what customers need and develop systems and processes that can respond on demand.

So why is it so difficult to create truly customer-focused service organisations capable of catering to the diverse needs of customers? Many organisations fail to comprehend that most of the work they perform does not create value for customers. There are many activities which are necessary in the provision of service but which are seen by the customer as hygiene factors or as correcting something that has failed to perform correctly. These are not value-creation activities.

We believe that the problem lies in changing the way people 'see' the nature of service work itself and in changing the way they think and behave in relation to customers. This requires a reorientation of workforce and management thinking that is as significant as changing humankind's thinking from an Earth-centred (self-centred) view of the cosmos, in which everything is seen as revolving around the Earth, to a Sun-centred cosmos, in which everything is seen as revolving around the Sun. The question organisations need to ask themselves, therefore, is this: do our customers have to spin around our business to get what they want?

Value chain definition

A customer value chain is not just an arrangement of organisational capabilities aligned end-to-end to perform what the company wants to perform, for example, marketing, sales, customer relationship management, service provision, billing, and service development. The real customer value chain weaves its way through these functions, overcoming many obstacles on the way.

Everything needs to be configured to allow the effortless consumption of goods and services when the customer wants them. This means removing all the hurdles, barriers and hoops customers need to navigate in order to experience and to put to good use the products or services they desire. Put simply, we need to make it easy for customers to 'pull' service.

We are part of a consumer-driven society, a world in which there is excess production capability, where competing on cost will no longer ensure survival; customers today demand services that cater to their needs. To differentiate themselves from the competition, therefore, companies are forced to offer more choice. And who can blame the customers for being choosier? A world with more choice, more variety and more diverse channels of delivery is a chaotic world both for organisations and for consumers.

Creating 'intelligence workers'

In such environments the skills of the 'knowledge worker' need to be applied not only in understanding the complexities of the products and services needed, but also in understanding the *customer* and the *context* in which the products and services are to be used. A service organisation needs not only to know the facts of the situation but to make sense of these facts in the context of the customer's world. We therefore need not just *knowledge workers* but *intelligence workers*.

Unless organisations rethink their way of operating and being, only those that operate in monopolistic circumstances will survive. *Sense and Respond: the Journey to Customer Purpose* describes how to take the first steps in redesigning the corporate infrastructure and in developing intelligence workers who not only understand customers deeply but also, with tools and techniques provided by this book, know how to diagnose problems in the corporate system. These staff then have the skills and the confidence to facilitate the systematic and continual evolution of an on-demand or 'pull' organisation.

Old ideas are failing to meet new demands

World markets and trends are ever-changing, and it is becoming increasingly difficult to survive competition from new providers who wish to compete on cost through the commoditisation of services.

In pursuit of achieving gains against the six business imperatives identified in Chapter 1, many support and service organisations respond in one of two ways:

1   they commoditise services through the use of automation and/or they transfer transaction activities to economies with low labour costs; or
2   they attempt to move up the customer value chain and to offer more services for which a premium can be charged.

There are a number of issues with each approach. Commoditisation, while improving cost-competitiveness, will ultimately lead the company into a long-term decline: the focus on costs will drive the pursuit of efficiency at the expense of effectiveness. This in turn will result in a loss of understanding of customers and of the organisational ability to adapt to changing customer needs.

Ascending the customer value hierarchy is possible only if the combined efforts of all operational teams are coordinated to provide adaptive processes, products and people (Holweg and Pil, 2004). In many cases where organisations are designed around functional specialisation, there is little or no capability to move rapidly up the value chain; the alternatives are to compete on cost or to commoditise the service.

A third option is to create an adaptive operation that is capable of permanently removing commoditised work. With this, the need to move work offshore or to invest in total automation can be avoided. Simultaneously, old services can be replaced with newly-identified value-added propositions. In order to achieve this, however, new principles upon which to design, build and operate organisations are needed. This in turn requires a new paradigm of management, quite different from traditional principles based on mass production.

Continuing to operate in the rigid 'make-and-sell' mode helps new competition steal the initiative from an organisation's customers and its future (Haeckel, 1999). The mass-production model worked well for Henry Ford and for most of the car industry in the 20th century when demand was unlimited. Huge benefits were gained through the reduction of unit labour costs driven by high-volume production. This held true for the early to middle 1900s. In a society in which over-capacity, global markets and workforces, commoditisation and greater consumer choice exist, competition through volume-driven strategies will eventually lead to extinction. Moving away from working to forecast volumes and towards working against actual demand calls for a different arrangement of delivery capabilities.

Organisations, having been driven to increase efficiency through volume, do not all see the logic of switching from mass production to Customer Value Principles: instead they continue to create products 'just in case' rather than 'just in time'. Many protest that abandoning the 'customer-push' model and moving towards a more responsive 'customer-pull' model would leave them open to the volatilities of seasonal fluctuations and indeterminate variable demand, which could cause havoc with scheduling and efficiency targets (Holweg and Pil, 2004). This very same argument, of course, demonstrates that current models are not designed to meet customer demand but rather to meet the operational efficiencies of the organisation. Most businesses plan and drive for efficient output, not for a new strategy for production.

Companies need to realise that optimising costs alone will not bring long-term profitability. The objective of businesses should be to provide the right product at the right time. Instead, major car companies, for instance, are joining forces in an effort to 'synergise' production capabilities and combine market share: this can be seen as a last attempt to keep in place an outdated strategy.

Growing leaner

Alternative approaches do exist. For over fifty years, Toyota has been working and continually developing what it calls the 'Toyota Production System'. Following World War II, the Japanese economy and infrastructure were completely devastated. Toyota therefore needed to find ways of doing more with less, and needed to create efficiency gains that were not based on volume. As a result Toyota developed a system known as *Lean Production*, and since then many companies around the world have tried to emulate it. Toyota's success in the auto industry is clear.

The on-demand, customer-pull system that is the central tenet of Lean Service is applied to the *entire value-creation chain* – from product design, through production, to delivery. A complete systematic change is required, whose premise should be the understanding that in order to create a highly responsive organisation, a new philosophy and mindset must be adopted.

With services as with manufacturing, the same mass-production thinking with its inherent problems has been applied to delivery. Diverse services, such as health care, public services, and even call centres, have been subjugated to this dogma. Implementation of improvement initiatives in such environments often leaves the business structure more rigid and less responsive to true customer needs. These actions represent a short-term fix; at best they yield results of 10–12 per cent on either cost-saving or efficiency measures. Case studies conducted on businesses that have adopted customer-pull principles, in contrast, show at least 30–40 per cent savings in efficiency or costs.

Customer service is often seen as a support function, as for example is after-sales in manufacturing. As a result, organisations have the misperception that the support being offered is at the *end* of the value-creation chain: it thus compensates for poor products and delivery, restoring lost value. Service at the very end of the delivery process is like quality measurements at the end of the production line: although a bad product has been identified, the organisation will still have incurred considerable direct and indirect costs. It has the expense associated with the production process, as well as the loss of potential revenue, customer goodwill and repeat business through production of a substandard offering.

A radical yet successful measure for organisations is to elevate call centres to management centres; or, even further from tradition, to make them responsible for the way the entire business performs end-to-end in front of customers. By tapping into the rich source of customer data that presents itself daily to frontline staff, the management centre can become the eyes and ears of the whole organisation, sensing what matters to customers and taking action.

In the provision of services there is an opportunity to do something different. Change is easier, because service-based businesses do not need to re-engineer production lines, relocate, or create detailed tooling specifications. The arena of customer service has long been recognised as the battleground for competition and the place to win customer loyalty. Why then do companies continue to deploy techniques of mass production when there are more responsive means to capture the hearts, minds and loyalty of customers?

Transform or mutate?

Most organisations slowly develop new services and products to maximise the current arrangement of assets and capabilities, using statistics based on what was previously understood as 'adding value'. Constrained by the current arrangement of operational facilities, business processes evolve and new solutions are predicated by previous ones. Through a gradual process, one service mutates into another; the organisation sees the seemingly improved service as optimal.

Changing relationships with customers

The present relationship between most organisations and their customers is a traditional one based on the production and consumption of goods and services that have been determined by marketing intelligence. The marketing departments of businesses are tasked with developing a process to persuade customers to buy these by stimulating demand for goods and services that the organisation has decided to push.

This approach is characterised as the 'make-and-sell' mode of operation (Haeckel, 1999): it is all about *customer push*. Manufactured products and the development of saleable services, however, both benefit if instead service organisations capture and exploit the customer demand intelligence that arrives every day. Marketing intelligence and focus-group data are not the only areas in which data can be collected; with a transformation in the staff's attitude, frontline operations, which are in a unique position to capture such data, can be tasked with attending to the real needs – not the *perceived* needs – of customers. Such an organisation can then make use of *customer pull* (Womack and Jones, 1996). Using this customer intelligence, the organisation can view its products and services, and potential new ones, from the vantage point of the customers who transact with it every day. Products and services can be specifically designed against what matters to the customer, and the business can also ensure that it operates at maximum effectiveness. Simply by locking on to customer demand intelligence presented to frontline operations, an organisation can continually satisfy its customers, create innovation, increase revenue, optimise costs, and provide meaningful work for frontline service staff.

This change in attitude depends on making the effort to understand the customer and get into his or her mindset. Once the organisation starts to take on the customer's viewpoint, the way in which it sees its own products and services will change, giving the organisation greater objectivity and enabling it to identify any shortcomings.

The need to transform

As with living creatures, organisations evolve to adapt to changes in their customer environments. Over time, some features mutate; over time, some businesses find that they cannot survive in the new conditions and become extinct. As customers become more demanding, only the fittest businesses survive. Some manage to keep going for a long time despite little internal change, but this lack of development renders them less flexible in responding to new demands: a sudden change in the business climate may reveal their inability to adapt. In contrast, the business that makes the effort to understand its own changing marketplace – the customer environment in which it lives – will find that this changing awareness actually triggers adaptation in response. The intelligent business therefore embraces voluntary evolution, designing its own fitness to survive and thrive.

The new and ever-changing desires of customers are given great attention, and many businesses vow that they are consumer-driven organisations. Usually, however, such organisations are 'inside-out' – corporately driven organisations that push products to maximise the use of current assets and capabilities (Womack and Jones, 1996). A truly consumer-driven organisation will design products and services from the customers' point of view, an 'outside-in' approach that requires a change in the current arrangement of assets and capabilities.

Customers require and demand more variety, and they can easily switch supplier in pursuit of innovative services and new products. In today's marketplace, few organisations are able to offer this level of variety or individuality in products and services. Any that can will have a distinct advantage in this type of market.

The key to successfully meeting the changing needs of customers is that businesses be responsive: that they commit themselves to delivering products and services identified by customer intelligence data. At the very least, the collection of such data allows decisions about whether or not to pursue new product lines to be *informed* decisions. By understanding customers' requirements and desires and allowing staff to 'pull' this intelligence, organisations can respond to customers' shifting demands.

A new customer request, identified and communicated to the organisation by frontline staff, may need to be considered by various departments; it may even require a third party to process it. In considering how best to respond to this new request, the organisation needs to consider each step of its own process and to ascertain whether or not this step adds value (Womack and Jones, 1996). By understanding how customer demand flows through a business, end-to-end, the organisation can discover whether it can truly satisfy customer needs *effectively* and efficiently.

To evaluate its ability to transform the business into one that truly delivers against the purpose of its customers, the business must first understand the pattern of work flow and how it creates or does not create value. It may seem that many organisations are far too complex or diverse for managers to begin to comprehend the intricacies of work flow. Understanding is made harder by the mutation of processes over time, and it can be hard to identify where to start gaining this understanding, let alone how to take action to improve things. We explain below how to set about this.

Understanding the origins of cost

In many service organisations, much of the demand that comes from customers is entirely preventable, and the consequent investment of time, effort, money and IT infrastructure is senseless. The make-and-sell solution simply makes preventable work move faster and imagines that this constitutes greater efficiency. This solution is ineffectual and fails to generate any value for the customer.

Understanding the *origins* of cost – that is, the factors that give rise to preventable demand – is therefore absolutely crucial. This too can be a challenge, however, if more than one department is involved: at worst, having several separate departments, each working to its own agenda, can actually increase the overall cost.

Developing a customer focus

Most businesses have split their operations and designed functional special-isations in separate departments. Many have individual targets and goals, with measurements related to specific outputs. Marketing departments endeavour to create demand so as to 'push' the products and services onto the customers.

In past decades this has been fairly successful, but is less so now. Customers currently want products and services that completely meet their needs. The old, familiar way of designing, building and operating organisa-tions cannot cope with the amount of customisation and variety that is being demanded.

Service and manufacturing businesses cannot afford to stockpile huge numbers of staff and varieties of products 'just in case' they are needed. Instead, organisations must consider new ways to create variety and indi-viduality, so that they can produce goods 'on demand' when the customer wants them (Womack and Jones, 1996). This requires a completely differ-ent mindset and leads to the physical reorganisation of the business, differ-ent business performance measurements, and the creation of a new Customer Leadership Culture that concentrates constantly on how to meet changing customer demands.

Creating customer success

Satisfaction and success

Customer satisfaction alone is insufficient; *customer success*, in which the goods or services exactly match the customer's perceptions and require-ments, must become the new focal point.

Most organisations, however, measure the success of their products and services by undertaking customer satisfaction surveys. The survey is usually introduced *after* the product or service has been experienced by the cus-tomer. Usually the survey collects only the information that the *organisa-tion* believes is important; and very few take into account the *context* in which the customer is using the goods or services. Currently, customer sat-isfaction is measured in terms of what the business believes it can deliver against, not in terms of creating customer success.

In order to sense the needs of customers and respond to these, an organi-sation should ask itself:

1 Why are customers using our products or services?
2 For what function are customers using them?

3   Do the products and services improve the customers' working environment?
4   Do they improve customers' personal lives?
5   Do they improve customers' professional lives?

The answers to these questions reveal the customer context in which products or services create value, and the extent to which customer success is or is not created.

In order to create true customer success, an organisation needs to deliver and measure against the outcomes of a product or service in relation to the customer context and customers' definition of value – not against internal, self-fulfilling functional statistics. Instead of making the primary measurements delivery time and specification, forward-thinking organisations should instead consider whether the product or service met the purpose for which it was purchased. It is at this point that *customer purpose* begins to be recognised.

Providing a new customer experience

When a business is designed around customer success, an improved customer experience is a natural outcome.

Many companies focus on making the customer's experience of transacting with the organisation both pleasurable and memorable. Many provide other features or benefits that compensate for deficiencies in the original product. This may maintain a certain level of customer loyalty, but the question that organisations really need to ask is more fundamental: should the customer be experiencing this interaction at all? Similarly, organisations invest an enormous amount of time and money in training personnel, implementing IT systems to handle enquiries, and administration costs to make the interaction a pleasant experience – yet a large proportion of service demand in an organisation is entirely preventable. What is the point of learning how to alleviate a situation routinely that could be prevented entirely? Improving the customer experience should not be aimed at making customers feel good about products or services that do not meet their needs. Instead, it should centre on delivering products that create customer success – and that create this success first time, every time. One of the earliest changes made by any organisation that starts to sense and respond to customer needs and purposes, before it makes efforts to improve the overall customer experience, is to eradicate unnecessary customer interactions and unwanted demand. Much of this unwanted demand is generated through earlier failures by the organisation and contribute to the overall cost of failure which must be borne by the organisation. *Only when this has been done* should the organisation move on to seeking to deliver to customer purpose and to questioning the very nature of the work or service provided. Put simply: *first* eradicate the obvious waste; *then* seek to create new value.

Although the mass-production model has served many organisations well for many years, businesses no longer need to function as they have traditionally. In business generally, and particularly in the service sector, this model has come to the end of its useful life, just as the propeller became obsolete when the jet engine was invented. The end of the mass-production model is not a disaster; already it is creating new opportunities, new markets, and – above all – a new future.

Organisational waste

> Whenever there is a product for a customer, there is a value stream. The challenge lies in seeing it.
>
> Rother and Shook (1999)

In factories and on building sites, waste can easily be seen. In pristine, ergonomically designed offices, however, the waste is less apparent. Yet it is nonetheless prevalent. Organisational waste is defined as: *all activity that does not contribute to the creation of customer value* (Womack and Jones, 1996).

From our own experience while introducing the Customer Value Principles to organisations, between 40 and 90 per cent of service demand is entirely preventable. Despite being unnecessary, however, this waste is locked in by organisational design or by processes that have mutated from their original designs and have become increasingly inefficient. Preventable work is often hidden and processed under the illusion that it creates value. Furthermore, many organisations fail to see the actual nature of preventable work, treating it as normal. As a result, demand becomes institutionalised and treated uniformly, irrespective of whether or not it adds value.

The journey to responsiveness is about first learning to see what actually creates value in an organisation and then acting on this new awareness. At this point, sadly, organisations may discover that many of their previous improvement efforts have in fact simply created 'neat waste'. In realigning an organisation to sense and respond, therefore, after the first step of committing the organisation to customer success through learning what creates value, the second step is to make waste visible.

The ghost of mass production past

Most businesses currently are hampered by a dominant management philosophy based on mass-production theory. This theory is so ubiquitous in literature and business schools that many managers and businesses are completely unaware of how pervasive it is. As a consequence, many managers quite instinctively create organisations built on mass-production principles.

This issue has been discussed many times by management commentators, but the work of Frederick Winslow Taylor's 'Scientific Management Movement', coupled with mass production, persists in most organisations. Taylor clearly believes that managers and workers are isolated entities. In *The Principles of Scientific Management* (1911), he states:

> It becomes the duty of those on the management's side to deliberately study the character, the nature and the performance of each workman with a view to finding out his limitations on the one hand, but even more important, his possibilities for development on the other hand.

Taylor claims that management should be separated from the work: that managers dictate and workers do. The manager, in this case, is forced to take on a parental role, determining how the work should be performed. In effect, this absolves the worker from any responsibility for creating innovation or improvement; and indeed Taylor describes a working environment in which innovative ideas and knowledge come only from the *top* of the organisational hierarchy.

The most significant and detrimental premise in Taylor's ideas is the assumption that performance levels are mostly attributable to individuals, not to the influences or constraints of the larger system within which they work. For Taylor, therefore, the managers' role is to pay attention to people – whereas in reality, as data reveals, managers need to pay attention to the *system* (Edwards Deming, 1982).

When the Scientific Management performance principles of 'one best way' joined forces with the functional specialisation of Henry Ford, the mass-production model was complete. Alfred Sloan at General Motors exemplified this thinking:

> Sloan thought it was both unnecessary and inappropriate for senior managers at the corporate level to know much about the details of operating each division. If the numbers showed that performance was poor, it was time to change the General Manager. General Managers showing consistently good numbers were candidates for promotion.
>
> Womack, Jones and Roos (1990)

This approach gave birth to what now is often called a 'silo mentality', whereby products and services are delivered by workers who know little or nothing of the work done by people in other departments, nor of the impact of their own work on colleagues or on the finished item. Mass production may be the most efficient means to hit a fixed target, but it is a totally inappropriate means to hit a moving one. Work is broken down into functional specialties and passed between departments. In each department, staff are focused on their own departmental goals, budgets and targets. In effect, organisations 'timeshare' demand, and thus customers. To *customers*, however, functional boundaries and departments are of little interest: what matters to them is whether value is created and delivered when they need it.

The 'functional specialisation' mentality may be obvious to cultures that were forced to create a different approach because of the resource constraints they faced, such as Japan after the Second World War. Konosuke Matsushita, founder of the Japanese electronic giant Matsushita, observes that Western firms are still inextricably linked to the paradigm founded upon Taylor's model. He continues:

> Even worse, so are your heads. With your bosses doing the thinking while the workers wield the screwdrivers, you're convinced deep down that this is the best way to run a business. We are beyond the Taylor model. Business, we know, is now so complex and difficult, the survival of the firm so hazardous in an environment increasingly unpredictable, competitive and fraught with danger that its continued existence depends on the day-to-day mobilisation of every ounce of intelligence.
>
> quoted in Crainer (1998)

Matsushita's philosophy emphasises the intelligence of the worker or, in services, of customer-facing staff.

The Theory-to-Performance Model

It has often been said that 'all models are wrong, but some are more useful than others'. Given this understanding, what follows is a model that demonstrates the relationships between management theory and performance, and which also provides a useful framework for discussion and for seeking consensus about which activities are actually undergoing transformation at any one time.

Any organisation needs to understand how management theories actually translate into frontline performance. The Theory-to-Performance Model is rooted in the belief that management theories can be distilled into a set of operating principles. These principles, as a result, condition management thinking about the design and shape of the organisation. Having settled on a design, an organisation sets goals, measurements and targets intended to drive the operation to focus on desired outcomes, which are deemed

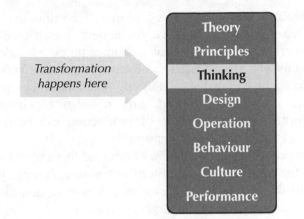

Transformation happens here

Theory

Principles

Thinking

Design

Operation

Behaviour

Culture

Performance

Figure 2.1 The Theory-to-Performance Model

effective because measurements and targets are known to influence heavily the behavioural characteristics of operating staff. The combined behaviour of teams and managers creates a corporate culture. When customers engage with the company, they interpret the collective effects of these elements in the form of delivery performance. Put simply, did the company effectively meet their needs?

The most important feature of the Theory-to-Performance Model (Figure 2.1) is that the design, operation, behaviour, culture, and ultimately, performance are emergent properties of the way people think. Sustained, cross-functional change with initiatives such as High Performing Teams, Six Sigma, TQM and Lean Production will not occur unless managers' thought processes have changed (Gharajedaghi, 1999). Otherwise, traditional thinking, mass-production targets and functional budgetary pressures will inevitably seep back into the organisation's design, driving managers and staff back into their safe space. Businesses that solely rely upon mass-production theories will have many 'silo issues' and will tend to look only for the next fad to fix these. Unless the underlying theory, principles and thinking change also, mass-production principles cannot and will not be eradicated (Seddon, 1992). Changing people's thinking is therefore the key point of leverage and thus the first challenge on the transformation journey.

Sustained focus on customer purpose

Delivering real value

Delivery operations must have clarity of purpose from the customer's point of view – all activities must contribute to the creation of customer value or customer success. Don't hurry this research. Take time to establish your customers' true purpose. Be sure that you understand what really matters to your customers – what is their real customer purpose? Unless you truly understand this, you may engage in well-meaning but ineffectual activity or find ways to do the wrong things 'righter'. When the real purpose is known and articulated, on the other hand, what needs to be changed becomes obvious. Further, relevant aspects of production can be measured and improvements can be made and monitored.

If service centres assess the nature of demand they currently receive and understand the context in which customers transact, they can gain a deeper insight as to the real needs of customers. A new organisational purpose coupled with new objectives and targets will emerge.

Imagine, for example, that you work in an IT services environment. Customers or end users call you to request urgent printer repairs. If you asked the customers what most mattered to them, their first reply might be: 'I need my printer repaired as quickly as possible.' As a result of a number of such experiences, your company, the service provider, might assume that solving issues as quickly as possible was important and might introduce targets and measurements related to this purpose. Service capabilities, training, job roles, reporting and processes would all be aligned to meet this objective.

However, the true customer purpose might actually be different. Suppose that when you received a call you took time to understand the context in which the transaction had been triggered. The *presenting* need appears to be to restore a printer to good order, but the *underlying* need might be to print theatre tickets, aircraft boarding passes, immigration documents, criminal records, medical records, sales proposals and shipping manifests. Getting the printer fixed was not the true purpose, which was simply to allow the customer to perform her duties. What really matters to her and to her customers is her ability to get on with her own work, which includes being able to print documents dependably and immediately. These are examples of requests or demands from customers to restore lost value.

If your company recognised this, it could choose instead to make problems and the prevention of them the focus of company performance at first. Might the supplier offer to upsell the customer a more versatile printer? Or to subcontract printing services? Thinking from a customer-purpose mindset, however, the supplier might instead look for innovative ways to eliminate the need for the printer at all by providing ticket-less solutions. Organisations should seek creative ways to eliminate the need to continually restore value and should pursue ways to create continuous value.

Staying open, staying flexible

Merely *knowing* your costs is life-threatening: *survival requires that you understand and work on the causes of cost.* If you understand the diverse environments in which your organisation's products and services operate, you can gain insight as to how they are really performing, and thus whether the product or service specification needs to be changed or whether new products or services need to be developed.

The idea of tracking diverse customer environments and situations may seem daunting, but it is eminently worthwhile. Later we will discuss how to understand the work of the customer-facing staff in your organisation and how to engage these staff in capturing and analysing customer intelligence so that your organisation can align itself purposefully. As mentioned already, this necessitates a different approach, a new role for frontline staff and managers, innovative performance measurements, and a new paradigm of service provision.

Here are some of the basic questions you should be asking of your organisation if you are seeking to implement Customer Value Principles:

1   What causes the customer to transact with the organisation?
2   Is the transaction necessary?
3   What is the real need and purpose behind the transaction?
4   What do I need to understand about the customer's context?
5   How is my organisation adding value and creating customer success?
6   Do I know how to start improving my organisation?
7   Am I just restoring lost value to customers, or am I seeking continuous customer value creation?

PART II

The Journey to Customer Purpose: Re-View

Introduction

Professor Daniel T. Jones
Chairman, Lean Enterprise Academy

Defining *value* correctly from the customer's perspective is the first principle of Lean Service. The second principle is to design and manage the whole process for delivering this value backwards from the customer, in a 'pull' system, rather than forwards from the assets the provider is seeking to keep busy. Most people have a hard time moving beyond eliminating waste from existing processes. However, these pioneering examples demonstrate just what can be achieved from being truly customer-focused.

The real significance of the authors' work is that it starts by understanding what the customer is trying to achieve – customer purpose – rather than from customer satisfaction or even customer delight. Through an informed and systematic dialogue with customers it is possible to enhance value and to eliminate the costs of unnecessary activities resulting from ineffective delivery process, system infrastructures and product designs. This sets in motion a virtuous circle from which both the customer and the provider continue to gain.

It also shows the way forward in creating more rewarding work in service organisations. In a Lean Enterprise work becomes much more purposeful, creative and meaningful, resulting in a dynamic culture – so people stay and grow. This provides the foundation for innovative service redesign and development.

CHAPTER 3

Re-View:
changing the point of view

Sensing what's important to customers

Current performance

Organisations that are capable of sensing what's important to customers and then engaging the resources of the entire organisation in response will always dominate the marketplace (Haeckel, 1999). The Re-View phase is not about reviewing things against what went before but about gathering together an 'outside-in' view of current performance, learning to sense what's important to customers, and measuring the end-to-end organisational response capability.

Organisations start to gain a deeper understanding of the *real* – as contrasted with the *perceived* – customer experience and also the nature of customer transactions. This new understanding presents the first indicators as to what needs to be measured and improved. Data from this perspective is later shared with everyone, end-to-end across the organisation. People begin to recognise and establish the new reality of service responsiveness from the customers' perspective.

This, however, calls for a shift in thinking and behaviour in terms of what people pay attention to. The total re-evaluation of the current organisational performance in relation to customer demand can sometimes lead to the realisation that instead of investing in previously identified customer groups or services, the organisation should perhaps be considering *other* customers or services.

This needs to be understood in context. Consider for a moment that most services being provided to customers are the result of things going wrong. This is rather like fixing tyres all the time, when in fact the cause of the problems (and thus the problem that really needs to be addressed) is bad roads. Many businesses will not look beyond the customer's presenting service request: 'I would like my tyres fixed.' Staying with the analogy, the business might then invest in tyre-fixing training and tyre-fixing equipment and

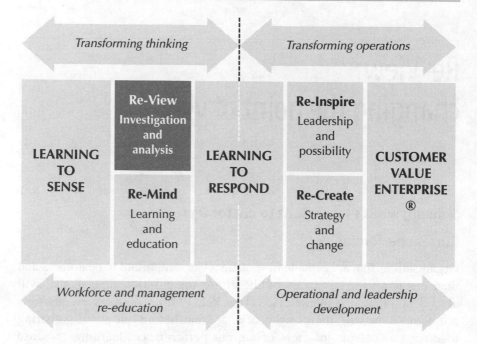

Figure 3.1 The Journey to Customer Purpose: Re-View

recruit the best tyre mechanics, when a better business solution would be to invest in road-building equipment and road-building training. And what happens to the tyre business if a competitor comes along and fixes all the roads?

As stated before, much of the demand that comes into service organisations is entirely preventable: it is caused by the organisation's own practices. On the face of it, it can seem logical to process all customer demand – endlessly to fit replacement tyres, and to suppose that this service has added value. But has it really added value given that the origin of the demand is the holes in the road – failures in the service provision itself?

It might be argued by some that although it is open to commercial enterprises to offer tyre changes (and even wheel replacements and balancing, and perhaps entire vehicle servicing, and so on), the 'failure in service provision' often lies outside the business's control. This seems like a plausible position to take, yet it raises an important question: 'Where, and to what extent, does the customer value stream flow?' Organisations working on Customer Value Principles first identify the *whole value stream*, examining their own role within it and looking for opportunities to extend their control, influence or partnership with others to ensure that value is created for customers.

The argument that 'It's some one else's responsibility' is often used to preclude any investigation into possible ways to extend the company influence. Many people within organisations are aware that the external components of the value chain do not work effectively and may even have a vested interest in keeping that way. The truth about how the value chain performs end-to-end often surfaces within organisations without action being taken. Winston Churchill once observed: 'Men occasionally stumble over the truth, but most of them pick themselves up and hurry off as if nothing has happened.'

Many organisations have within their own business the data that would at least allow them to investigate the possibilities of extending the value chain, but they fail to take action because they have abdicated that responsibility to other organisations, agencies and institutions, or worse still, to their competitors.

Matching performance to customer purpose

Were you to investigate customer purpose, you might discover that although fixing tyres quickly mattered to customers, the underlying value to them was to be able to travel to their destination. In other words, when you see the world from the customer's perspective, your marketplace will become much bigger and will be full of previously unrecognised opportunities. Understanding what customers really want allows you to provide services that will really assist them in their purpose. In the example given, an understanding of what value means from the customer perspective – the ability to reach a chosen destination – might lead your organisation to decide to begin building its own roads or mending the bad roads of its competitors, or to recruit driving instructors to demonstrate to customers how to get more value out of their vehicle, or to employ staff to help customers determine their best routes, the best time of day to travel, and activities of interest to the customer on arrival at the chosen destination.

Two options exist for businesses: *to make offers to customers* or *to respond to customers' needs*. The shift in thinking from restoring value – fixing it when it has gone wrong – to thinking about *continuous value creation* creates infinite possibilities, limited only by imagination and by the current design of the organisational system.

Commitment to identifying customer purpose

How and where do organisations begin to understand the current state of their performance through the eyes of their customers? This is achieved by scrutinising all interactions and analysing them from the customer's viewpoint.

> Companies today must be driven by a deep understanding of changing customer needs.
>
> Haeckel (1999)

All organisations *purport* to want to understand their customers, yet many are wary of looking closely at how they are serving or not serving their customers. It may be an uncomfortable thing to do and could prove to be disruptive, threatening a host of existing investments and power structures.

But brave and aspirational companies know that they need to do this anyway. They look at themselves unwaveringly through the eyes of their customers and keep their focus, whatever they see. The more they see, the more they learn to look; and this shift in thinking lends itself to a change of culture in which fears about discussing service failures gradually dissolve and traditional management practices are broken down.

Seeing the organisation as a system

In thinking about your organisation, you need to keep in mind that not just the *actions* but also the *interactions* are important. To begin to define the reality of service provision as seen through the eyes of customers, organisations must first learn to understand their end-to-end structures as *one system* (Gharajedaghi, 1999).

All of the organisational functions, all of the 'corporate plumbing' that joins them together, the environment in which the customers operate and the environment in which the organisation operates together comprise *one system*. What is crucial is the way in which all of these parts interact – not just the way that any one part works, but how they all work together and the system dynamics that this working together creates (Beer, 1994).

A business system model

The simple business system model in Figure 3.2 illustrates the interactions and dynamics of the environment the organisation needs to evaluate.

Market and competition conditions

The organisation needs first to understand its own marketplace, its trends and emerging services, together with an overview of competitors'

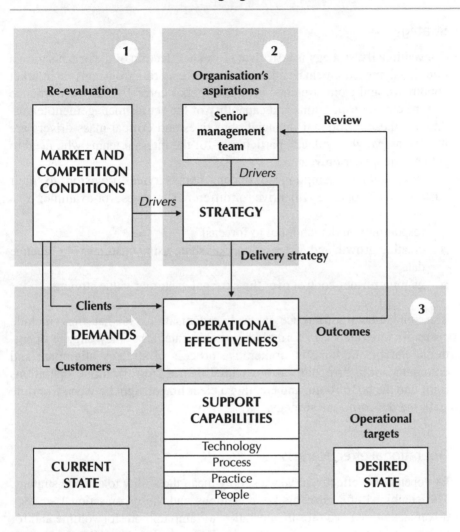

Figure 3.2 A business system model

movements and strategies. But this is just the beginning. To create real differentiation in the market, the organisation needs to capture intelligence about current customer needs and trends. Customers are demanding new value daily.

Can your organisation capture that kind of intelligence? It needs to, because these understandings ought to be the drivers that determine the organisation's strategic intent and thus allow it to set objectives.

Strategy

Conventionally, strategy is articulated from a reflection of the organisation's traditional measurements and performance criteria, from current market conditions, and from stretched growth targets steered by past performance and the current aspirations and capability of the senior management teams. At best, these traditional financial objectives and critical-mass drivers are just 'what everybody does', particularly for the internal teams who need to achieve them year on year.

Organisations attempting to match their service provision to their customers' perspective will strive for different strategies, for example:

- responding on demand, not to forecast
- creating growth and increased market share using customer intelligence data
- gaining further control over the external customer value stream.

The fundamental difference in such organisations is that they include customer intelligence in formulating their strategies – they engage operational staff in the continuous iterative process of strategy alignment and communication, bringing customer intelligence from frontline operations right into the boardroom, and creating a clear line of sight between frontline staff and the corporate strategy.

Operational effectiveness

By 'operational effectiveness' we simply mean the ability to execute strategy. The combined effects of market conditions and the organisational strategy drivers result in a need for the operation to ramp up both for volume and for complexity in response to the demands of diverse customers. Operations will determine, by capturing the profile of incoming customer demand, whether the current operational model is capable of providing and sustaining the goods or services customers are trying to pull from the organisation. They will also examine the underlying support structures of technology, people, processes, practice and policy within the context of the profile of customer demands.

To be able to understand how all these elements of the business system interact, an organisation needs to ask itself the following questions:

- How does our current system perform, from the customer's perspective?
- What is important to our customers?
- Why do they use our services?
- In what context and environment do our customers operate?

- What analysis techniques will be deployed to gather and understand this intelligence?
- How can we capture and analyse customer demand?
- How can operational effectiveness and efficiency be measured against profiles of demand?
- How do we apply new customer measurements to the entire service delivery chain?

When the organisation is analysed as a system, it becomes possible to identify where remedial action can be taken. But it is vital that organisations make a detailed analytical map before effecting any change (Gharajedaghi, 1999). This can be likened to treating a person who is unwell. First diagnostic tests can be carried out to identify what ailment the patient is suffering from; subsequently remedies may be prescribed. Self-inflicted ailments might necessitate a complete change in lifestyle. If, as may happen in some instances, the ailment has an external cause, it may be necessary to address the environment in which the person lives or works. Indeed, in many cases both actions will be required.

Investigating the system

The lean practitioners' toolkit

Many of the analytical tools used in the Re-View phase can be found in the Lean Practitioners' toolkit – there are many good books that detail their use. Below we mention several techniques that are particularly useful in understanding how the organisation responds to customer purpose and that aid in identifying organisational constraints.

We must emphasise, however, that transformation is not found in the use of tools, but in grasping and applying the concepts. There must be thinking and purpose behind their use, and this is the focus of the Re-View stage. Indeed, unless their use is accompanied by a change in theory and thinking, using 'lean' tools might actually make matters worse – it is not the tools that perform the transformation but the minds that use them. The purpose of analysis is not to master tools but to gain insight (Womack and Jones, 1996).

Mapping the system

Two kinds of mapping will prove useful to an organisation learning to sense and respond:

- **Value Stream Mapping.** A simple diagram is made that shows every step involved in the creation of value for the customer from making a choice, service or order initiation, through to delivery, consumption and disposal (Womack and Jones, 2005).

- **System Mapping**. A diagram is made that provides information on the relationship between company strategies, client strategies, organisational structures, system constraints, HR practices, reward and recognition systems, IT infrastructure, and any other factors that impact the value stream (Gharajedaghi, 1999). The basic structure replicates that found in the Customer Value Enterprise® (see Chapter 11).

The customer viewpoint as a point of reference

Analysing the system may seem daunting as the system is multilayered, multidimensional and interdisciplinary. In order to understand complex systems, both a common point of reference and a systematic investigation process are required (Gharajedaghi, 1999). Commonly organisations that attempt this try to understand their own complexity starting from the viewpoint of their corporate values, their behaviour, their process or their finance. *Our* point of reference, relative to which we can assess and understand the complex nature of organisational interactions, is the *customer*. The customer viewpoint will become the measure of value of all service and will determine the impact of transactions.

Analysis will show whether the system is actually *connected* to customers. Most organisations exist to serve customers, to make a profit and to provide meaningful jobs for their employees, yet without making the changes that allow the system continually to work effectively for the customer, many of these businesses will be unable to achieve those goals.

The most successful approach we have found when analysing the system is to involve people who represent a cross-functional, cross-hierarchical slice of the organisation, including representatives of all the support functions that currently provide customer service, from the frontline and through management (Gharajedaghi, 1999). This group will understand how to view the organisation from a customer perspective; more importantly, they will have acquired the skills, experience and methods to work continually with new techniques and to drive essential actions.

Learning to apply new techniques to gather data related to what's important to customers and presenting the view of the organisation's capability to respond, while important, do not in themselves create transformation. Transformation comes from understanding the data from a different perspective, from applying a different set of principles and thinking, and then from taking action on the system (Seddon, 1992). You can only transform the business after you have transformed the mindsets.

Collecting real data

A word of caution: as in any investigative process, the people who ask the questions have a tendency to collect only the data that agrees with their viewpoint or their expectations. Investigative team members need to be sure that they have learned to set aside their personal prejudices and perceptions so that they can engage others in conversation and enable freedom of expression without manipulation or coercion.

To test this now, ask yourself what you were thinking as you just read the previous two sentences. Were you truly focused on the text? Or were you thinking about something else? For example, you might have been thinking about:

- what you thought about what was written
- how you could have written it better
- why you didn't agree with what was written
- how you could relate it to your own situation ...

And so on.

Data collated from customer surveys is often disappointing and may reveal nothing that isn't known already. Often this is because the organisation has unconsciously been looking only for data it knows how to deal with, even though this does not uncover the true state of service provision. So remember: if you truly wish to collect data that will tell you the truth about your organisation, learn how to be truly cognisant of what's important to the other person – *don't just focus on what you want to hear*. Even more importantly, *don't assume that you know your customers*. What may seem obvious and able to be taken for granted might turn out to be completely wrong.

Customer purpose defines customer value

It is easy to become confused about what matters to customers and to lose sight of real purpose. This sometimes leads to well-meaning activity focused on doing 'business as usual, only better'. However, unless the real purpose is known and articulated, it cannot be measured and therefore no improvements can be made.

Measurement can clearly make improvement more precise, but it is not always essential. For example, if you manufactured china and much of it was broken in transit to the shop, you wouldn't need a *measurement* of the breakage to know that you could make some improvement simply by packing the china more securely. However, in the case of Office Products Direct Europe (see Chapter 12) it was only through measurement that the inadequacy of the packaging for electronic equipment was discovered. Even though personal computers were being returned broken and customers were complaining, it never occurred to the staff or managers who processed the returns to initiate an investigation. Why not? Simply because it was not perceived as their job to do so, and because the number of broken PCs was low relative to the total number of returned items they needed to process.

Sometimes the most obvious failures go unreported because people feel that someone else who has the responsibility must surely be aware of the problem and it needs no further action. If they do not deal directly with the customer themselves, they also may not appreciate the impact for the customer of minor failures.

What is important and what matters?

There is a subtle but distinct difference between what *matters* to customers and what is *important* to them. For example, it may matter to a customer that a product is delivered on time, but what's important is that the product is what they ordered and will function in accordance with the use to which they put it. A frequently used example is the purchase of an electric drill. What *matters* to the customer is that the product functions correctly on demand, but what is *important* is that it drills holes in the wall. Is the customer purchasing an electric drill or holes in a wall? Taking this thought further, once the organisation understands what is important to customers and to what purpose they put their products, the organisation can look at innovative ways of creating either the same value or added value without being restricted to providing the product or service they provided in the past.

To understand the true customer purpose you need to understand the *context in which the transaction takes place*, which will give clues to the real purpose. This refers to the customer's experience when dealing with the service provider.

- What does the transaction look like from their perspective?
- What are the business outcomes if there's a failure in service for the customer?
- What are the indirect impacts on the customer's customers?

In their book *Lean Thinking: Banish Waste and Create Wealth in Your Corporation* (1996), James P. Womack and Daniel T. Jones ask why organisations have such difficulties in identifying value. Their response, which is as applicable to service as it is to manufacturing, is this:

> Partly because most producers want to make what they are already making, and partly because many customers only know how to ask for some variant of what they are already getting.

This point is so crucial that it must be emphasised: *without understanding customer purpose, any discussion about customer value will be futile.*

A common misconception in business is that it is sufficient to deliver services only to a set specification that meets customer needs. To an extent, of course, this can be true: customers often do buy a particular product or service but that may be because it is the only one on offer – usually a variant of what is already being produced, not something customised. So how does an organisation establish whether the customer genuinely *needs* its products or services?

Put simply, meeting customer purpose means delivering what's *important* to the customer – not necessarily what is already produced to specification, and not necessarily just on time. Value differs for every customer; each has different purposes and different needs. At the outset, therefore, the application of Customer Value Principles can seem daunting or even impossible to achieve. Through analysis, however, organisations can see what is common to groups of people and design against these different groups.

When an organisation knows what its outputs are and what uses they are put to, customer relationship management (CRM) tools are traditionally used to push those stockpiled products to market. The organisation uses CRM tools to identify lifestyles and opportunities in order to sell customers something that the customers may already have or do not need. This is 'push-CRM', the main concept of a make-and-sell approach. We advocate using the very same tools, but with the data flow in a completely different direction, starting from an understanding of the purpose for which products are needed by an existing customer base.

This point can be illustrated by describing two approaches to car sales. The first is the traditional 'push' approach. A car showroom stocks various cars in greens and blues. A customer who asks for his favourite colour, red, is instead induced to purchase from among what is on offer, either green or blue. The customer decides that the discount offered is enough for him to purchase a green car, even though he was prepared to pay full price for his chosen car in red. This sale, like all the others, is recorded on the inventory system. When the sales data are analysed later, the manufacturers are are likely to conclude, 'Hey – these green cars are doing well – let's make some more!' Although this might be perceived as success, it is not as successful as it *could* have been.

Now the 'pull' approach. If car sales are made on this system, the result is the reduction of inventory waiting to be sold. More red cars are available because the data is more accurate. There is no requirement to offer discounts, which is the source of significant corporate waste. Additionally, the customer buys what he actually wants and is willing to pay the full price for it and sometimes to wait longer for it. And because the inventory is much lower, costs are lower, so the manufacturer or service provider has a healthier bottom line.

Demand classification

All work is a process and must be subject to constant improvement. In today's rapidly changing world, the nature of demand from customers is changing also. Only by constantly improving processes can organisations genuinely put their customers first. Where processes are unsuited to the needs of the customer, the service experience always worsens and costs rise (Seddon, 1992). Customers can sense when organisations are sticking to ill-fitting processes or scripts rather than solving their problems. In order to align business processes to the needs of customers, a demand classification system is required.

Once a service organisation has developed a method for identifying the nature of customer demand and has the ability to measure its response, it will find it far easier to recognise new demands and to react accordingly. It follows that any organisation with effective process management is better positioned to deal with rapid change and to maximise the potential return from its customers.

At the heart of the diagnostic approach, therefore, is the unique classification of customer demand. Most companies wish to create value for their customers and sincerely believe that their customer-service operations are indeed doing that. On closer inspection, however, it may turn out that a significant proportion of incoming service demand is not actually creating value at all, but just restoring value. We therefore classify customer demand into two types: demand that is created from *positive* origins, and demand that is *negative* or *restorative* in its origins. Identifying the proportion of positive to negative demand is an integral part of improving services and reducing operating costs.

Positive and negative customer demands each have two sub-components, as shown in Figure 3.3: creation and opportunity demands, both positive; and restorative and external demands, both negative.

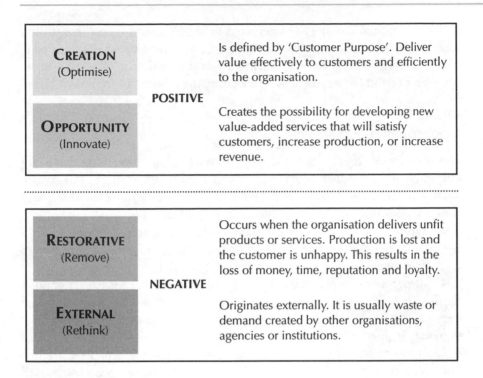

CREATION (Optimise)	**POSITIVE**	Is defined by 'Customer Purpose'. Deliver value effectively to customers and efficiently to the organisation.
OPPORTUNITY (Innovate)		Creates the possibility for developing new value-added services that will satisfy customers, increase production, or increase revenue.
RESTORATIVE (Remove)	**NEGATIVE**	Occurs when the organisation delivers unfit products or services. Production is lost and the customer is unhappy. This results in the loss of money, time, reputation and loyalty.
EXTERNAL (Rethink)		Originates externally. It is usually waste or demand created by other organisations, agencies or institutions.

Figure 3.3 CORE Demands

Creation demand

Creation demand comes into a service organisation because customers want to understand how to optimise the functionality of their service or product, or how to obtain more of what they already have. Creation demand is not the result of something being wrong, but rather the result of customers' questions such as: 'Which product is best?' or 'How can I get more out of my product or service?'

For efficient delivery, creation demand must be optimised (Womack and Jones, 1996). This is the type of demand that the organisation wants to keep, so the organisation needs to make it simple and easy for the customer to 'pull' service. Identification and analysis of how the end-to-end processes deliver against this demand type will indicate clearly which elements of the support structure could be improved, for example using tools for automation or web-based assistance.

Creation demand is seen in many service sectors. Customers of a bank, for example, may wish to gain more information from their bank statements and transactional details, to understand how they could better invest their existing savings, or to find out in which countries they could use their bank cards. Similarly, customers enquiring about their utilities may wish to set up a direct debit for payment or to ascertain the amount of their next bill.

Opportunity demand

Opportunity demand occurs when the customer wants something that is not currently offered. Most organisations will merely apologise to customers, saying that they can't fulfil the demand, and will then terminate the transaction. In a customer-centric organisation, in contrast, it is critical to capture these types of enquiries as they can provide a rich source of ideas and data for new services or product lines. Opportunity demand needs innovation to create new services and potential revenues need to be explored.

Consider as a simple illustration an independent burger bar. If enough demand is created for a specific burger topping, then the business can adapt very quickly and just add this topping to the menu so that it can now meet demand. If, however, several people request not burgers but pizzas, these customers present an opportunity. The outlet may not sell pizza currently, but over a period of time, in a completely unscientific way, the owner will recognise the sustained demand for pizza. The owner may have 'drilled down' and even identified that these requests arise on a particular day of the week. When the demand reaches a significant proportion, the burger bar owner will offer pizzas for a limited trial period. It may happen that there is little take-up, and pizza will then be withdrawn again. Or it may happen that the demand for pizza grows and eventually outstrips the demand for burgers. Having made an informed decision, the business may then swing around to become a pizza outlet rather than a burger outlet.

Restorative demand

Restorative demand occurs when the organisation delivers unfit products or services, generating unwanted demand as a consequence. This causes customer dissatisfaction, resulting in loss of money, time, reputation and loyalty.

The work involved in correcting this situation is deemed to be restoring lost value. In the eyes of the customer, restoring value is seen as: '*You* broke it, *you* fix it!' Restorative demand needs to be removed by identifying and rectifying the originating cause, which may reside in other parts of the organisation. Only in poorly run or unethical companies would you find revenue being generated against demand of this type.

Restorative demand becomes a drain on resources, and ineffective organisations inadvertently generate between 40 and 90 per cent of the total customer demand in this negative way. Here's a golden rule: *never automate this restorative demand.* Automation locks in frustration for the customer as well as for the frontline staff whom the customer has to call repeatedly about the organisation. Support staff also feel disenfranchised because existing constraints prevent them from making any difference in this situation. The spiral continues, with the customer becoming more and more disillusioned, which generates additional negative demand. All the while, the frontline staff feel powerless to change things.

External demand

External demand is failure generated externally by other agencies, institutions or companies. Organisations can generate revenue against this type of demand as long as it continues to present itself – that is, until a competitor (to return to the earlier example) fixes the road and removes the need to fix tyres.

External demand should be addressed by rethinking the environment that allows it to exist and by developing new solutions. In this context it is perfectly respectable to restore value, because the other things that are not working are the responsibility of other people. In fact, some businesses are set up specifically to handle this type of demand. However, organisations with this business model have to question the basis of their future: are the revenues that they are generating largely dependent on other companies failing to perform their duties? If so, what happens if those companies start performing well? This business model can be fundamentally flawed, depending on how exposed the business is and whether or not it is totally dependent on restoring value as a revenue stream.

CORE in action: an example

Once demand has been classified, each type needs to be treated in an appropriate way. Most organisations do not separate types of demand and treat all demand in the same way, as units of work to be processed efficiently (Seddon, 1992). In many cases organisations have automated all their demand, including the restorative type, thereby institutionalising waste. This approach can be very seductive. At face value, it it does indeed reduce costs but it disguises the reality that the organisation is automating work that it could actually remove.

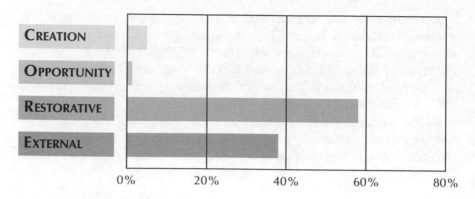

Figure 3.4 Demand-type breakdown

Figure 3.4 shows the distribution of demand types received by an international telecommunications company that supports internet and broadband customers. Approximately 300,000 enquiries are received every month. These enquiries are due to one of three principal causes:

1 Problems with the provision of internet services.
2 Consumers experiencing problems with their own equipment, such as personal computers.
3 Consumers requiring additional services or enhancements.

Analysis shows the following:

■ 57 per cent of the demand is generated when consumers experience a problem with the supplier's internet infrastructure (restorative demand).
■ Another 38 per cent originates from the customer's equipment (external demand). A significant proportion of this demand includes revenue opportunities currently not considered.
■ 4 per cent represents demand that provides a real potential to add value to consumers' experience, including increasing their bandwidth or helping them use their broadband connection for new purposes (creation demand).

Ongoing revenue from connecting customers to the network has only a limited lifespan; future revenue has to come from providing greater content and services, as well as enhancing and expanding existing usage.

The current support philosophy is to design against problems, and needs to change to a philosophy that removes root causes and provides value to customers in an effort to change the demand profile.

The current demand profile, with 4 per cent creation demand and 1 per cent opportunity demand, demonstrates the effect on customers of the current approach.

CHAPTER 4

Re-View:
end-to-end effectiveness

Seeing the organisation end-to-end

Understanding the CORE Demand profile is just the first step. Understanding and measuring how the organisation responds end-to-end is the next important activity.

Value is created for customers by the entire end-to-end organisation. Understanding how the combined efforts of all departments and teams contribute to creating value is therefore essential to understanding where organisations undertake unnecessary work and where they are aligned or misaligned to meet customer needs.

Measuring the right things

The organisation needs a new concept of measuring its service – not just from the functional-specialisation point of view, but by calculating the whole end-to-end system. What we are advocating is looking at the entire organisation as one block, ignoring the departmentalisation and reviewing the organisation's entire performance.

End-to-end effectiveness measurements are not the same as *efficiency-related output measurements*. Output measurements – such as 'the number of calls answered' or 'total sales' – may indicate a problem exists but do not specify what to do about it. End-to-end measurements indicate how well any system responds to demand. For example, an end-to-end measurement might indicate that 'Whenever a particular request is made, it always takes approximately 1 hour plus or minus 15 minutes to respond'. Similarly, in an online environment a typical end-to-end measurement could be 'The elapsed time from order taken to final delivery'. Provided that there is no change to the system and no unusual occurrences, end-to-end effectiveness measurements predict how well organisations will respond.

Once the elapsed time for delivery is known, a company can make an informed decision about whether or not it wants to improve this. If changes to the system are made, the same end-to-end measurement can be used to gauge the effectiveness of that change. When the organisation's focus is on the end-to-end measurement, people in the system begin to learn and understand which factors influence service. Once an effective system is in place, the organisation can set about optimisation.

By tracking the end-to-end measurements over time, it is possible to identify the typical processes, procedures, practices, dependencies and bottlenecks that continuously cause deterioration to service. Collectively, these types of failures are referred to as the *common causes of variation* (Edwards Deming, 1982). They are common to the way systems have been designed, implemented, and operated. If something out of the ordinary occurs, it is usually due to a *special* cause. The ability to separate special causes from common causes of variation in performance is fundamental to system management. Unless a company is planning for contingencies, it makes little sense to implement procedures or processes for events that are neither controllable nor predictable.

Identifying causes of service variation

Some of these causes may be, for example, out-of-stock items, poor product or service information, slow IT systems that inhibit performance, service delivery failures, poorly trained staff, lack of system definition, and organisational gaming (the practice of sticking to the letter of the law because that makes the numbers, rather than achieving the organisation's principal purposes). In such an environment, collecting data is key to improving both customer and employee satisfaction while also addressing the need of the organisation to make a profit. Once the data is obtained, it is imperative that the company use it to make the necessary changes, and then use the end-to-end measurements again to check that service has improved.

When measuring how well the organisation creates value for the customer, managers and especially staff need to look carefully at *all* of the data, as this will not only show the *average* performance but, much more usefully, where to improve. The data contains valuable information that can help them improve customer experience and create success and reduce costs.

Capability of means measurements

An easy parallel with an organisation's capability of means measurements (Johnson and Bröms, 2001) is the capability of a car. A given car may be capable of doing 50 miles to the gallon, but it will not do that on every journey, primarily because the conditions vary. It will *never*, however, do

70 miles to the gallon under any circumstances – this is simply beyond its capability. Similarly for an organisation: if a customer is asking for more than the capability you know your organisation can deliver, you know and can reliably predict that you will not be able to satisfy that customer.

Through the measurement of the end-to-end system, organisations are able to identify any weaknesses and can concentrate on improving the outputs in those areas for the good of their customers.

A simple example will illustrate predictability of performance. Consider what causes variation in the time to travel to work. A person might say it takes her, on average, between 20 and 30 minutes to drive to work. Sometimes the journey is quicker, and sometimes it takes longer. The best and worst times for this journey together show the *range* of travel times. This range can result from variation caused by the driver herself, or by external circumstances some of which may be unpredictable.

If she reflected on what caused the range, the driver might understand that on some days she had got to work in 15 minutes when the roads were clear and she drove above her usual speed. On days when it took much longer she had encountered traffic jams; journeys that took unusually long times had involved delays caused by accidents.

Delays that are predictable can be considered to be part of the 'system' of travelling to work: in this case the causes of variation are common to the system and are called *common causes of variation*. Only when causes are *predictable* should the driver create strategies either to exploit or to avoid the circumstances that impact journey time. The other circumstances that affect the travel time, which are outside the control of the driver and are completely *unpredictable*, are referred to as *special causes of variation*.

Organisations must learn to separate common-cause variation from special-cause variation. Having identified which is which, the organisation can then work on removing the *common* causes of variation – the internal factors that cause delays and increase waste, such as untrained staff, inappropriate processes, and inappropriate practices. Removing these causes reduces the range of variation in relation to system performance as a whole, so system performance becomes much more predictable.

A point that is often overlooked is that if an organisation simply uses statistical analysis to create an average, it will not be able to manage and predict performance because of these fundamental errors of ignoring the range of performance and including special causes. This approach might be likened to having one foot in molten lava and the other in liquid nitrogen and declaring that 'on average' you should feel comfortable!

If you measure your business on averages, don't be surprised to find yourself running an average business! Only when your organisation has identified the type, volume and frequency of demand can it start to take action. When it understands the causes of variation, it can begin to reduce the range of variation, and thus improve the predictability of the overall performance (Edwards Deming, 1982).

Measuring variation in performance

Using control charts to measure capability

Understanding and removing the causes of variation is the key to improving business performance. *Control charts* were developed in the 1920s by Walter A. Shewhart to provide details on the performance and capability of business process. Control-chart techniques are simple and powerful, and in the hands of the intelligence worker they can be turned into drivers for change.

The key advantage of using control charts is in establishing the difference between the *performance factors* that form part of the delivery system and the *external factors* that lie outside the system. The control chart thus assists in identifying performance variation that is inherent in the system as distinct from that caused by external factors. Unless the data can be separated out, external factors could be wrongly attributed to employees, for whom inappropriate targets might then be set based on these misleading numbers. In addition, the system has its own internal variability which occurs simply from the design of the business process.

When applied to the end-to-end system, control-chart techniques will provide the organisation with what we call *capability measurements*. Consider the example of a company wishing to understand the end-to-end capability of its organisation to deliver parcels on time. Suppose it found that it had a mean success rate of just 68 per cent, but that the variation around this mean was quite wide-ranging – from 57 per cent to 80 per cent. Asking staff to improve on the mean figure of 68 per cent would just result in everyone trying harder. What is needed is to understand the *causes* of variation in the delivery system and to rectify these.

Insights from capability measurements

A control chart will reveal much about the organisation, some of which may be startling. This may lead to the realisation that the organisation can take an extraordinarily long time to fulfil a simple request. It is not unusual at this stage for the organisation to discover, for instance, that it sometimes takes ten days to do a ten-minute job, just because the system was designed that way. Waste has been built in, and treated as if it were normal.

Understanding the system interactions

For all of these situations it is important to understand and define the environment, the conditions, and the behaviours created for the customer, as well as for the external suppliers and the people within the organisation who deal with customer transactions. As part of the analysis, information needs to be revealed that answers these questions:

- How do managers and staff behave?
- What do managers and staff pay attention to?
- How are managers and staff measured?
- What happens when customers can't use the service?
- What is important to customers?

This information will help to determine not only how to present data in a way that colleagues will respond to favourably, but also – and more importantly – how to identify the critical aspects of what may *constrain* transformation activity, and thus what could *release* it.

This is not the usual approach adopted by organisations. Most have detailed approaches for capturing, sifting and presenting this data with the use of technologies and best practice. Although managers can glean some trends from such information, the result is only scratching the surface. What makes the difference is gaining insight into the context in which the demand is generated.

'Reality shock' and the beginning of transformation

Identifying the CORE Demand profile exposes the significant amount of demand coming into an organisation that does not create value. It makes little commercial sense to spend resources in creating an expedient flow for this demand type: it is far better, wherever possible, to eradicate it. This is why it is vital to be able to recognise and differentiate between the four CORE Demand types (Figure 4.1).

Reactions to this new understanding of the profile of demand tend to be expressions of surprise, and can include the following:

- 'We thought we understood our customers and were customer-centric.'
- 'We thought that everything joined up fairly well end-to-end.'
- 'We thought our "fix" targets were being met and we were doing well.'
- 'We thought we had a common mission.'
- 'We thought because we had best practice we must be doing OK.'

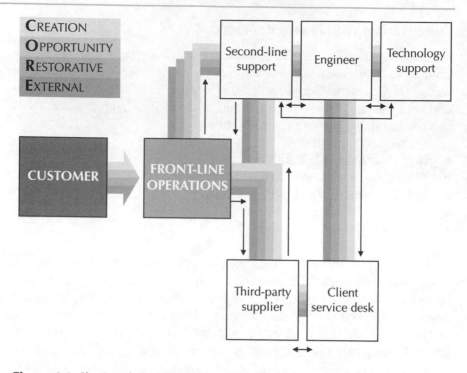

Figure 4.1 Sharing the profile of demand

- 'We found delivering only to specification was not enough.'
- 'We were creating value, but for only 10 per cent of the time.'

Another shock may result from this new awareness of reality and is perhaps more profound. The organisation may come to realise that although it has spent years investing a huge amount of money in developing new products and in changing the way the organisation fits together to meet the needs of the customers, the current organisation meets neither the customer requirements nor the customer purpose.

This realisation can have a dramatic impact. In extreme circumstances the new reality can send tremors through the organisation, especially when the organisation is one that impacts on the social environment surrounding it – as might be the case for an organisation delivering social services, health services or immigration services, for example. The effect can be likened to putting the lights on at a good party, and revealing all the mess – an action often greeted with cries of 'Turn the lights off! We were enjoying ourselves!' This is the point of choice for the organisation: the more dramatic the shock of realisation, the more necessary it is that the organisation not turn a blind eye but take its first steps toward transformation.

Investigation and analysis

Stages

The following stages of investigation and analysis may appear similar to other types of activities, but the purpose is quite different – this is not about trying to improve on current designs of system processes, but about establishing how current designs perform against customer purpose. They also create a new measuring system related to customer value. The baseline data yielded by this investigation and analysis will be used to track all future progress, create new operational governance and reporting systems, and lay down the foundation for long-term cultural transformation and operational development.

Here are the four stages that have proved effective. (They are exemplified in the case studies in Chapters 12 and 13.)

■ **Getting the team together**. Ensure that internal sponsorship, high-level support and back-up resources are in place to free up the investigation team. Gain agreements.

■ **Mapping constituencies**. Identify the areas, activities and departments that may influence the flow of value through the organisation. Identify key processes, products, information and constraints.

■ **Investigating the current state**. Use the analysis tools described above to collect statistics of performance variation, devise control charts, and implement capability measurements.

■ **Presenting findings and data**. Present findings and data to senior management teams prior to the Re-Mind phase.

Maintaining organisational change

Chapters 5 and 6 outline the crucial requirement for reorientation and for learning Transformational Leadership techniques that maintain organisational change and continuous improvement. Sustained commitment to improvement is a fundamental aspect of transformation if you aim to keep up the momentum of change. Leadership, mentoring and coaching need to focus on the way people think and behave, challenging assumptions and traditional practices, and breaking through conventional thinking and mental models. Learning to have leadership conversations in which analysis data can be shared freely further catalyses change and creativity, leading to a powerful spiral of inspiration and growing tenacity for change. As we go on to outline examples of the diagnostic approach, remember that this is accompanied by a set of theories, principles and Transformational Leadership techniques.

As noted before, the fundamental shift in an organisation that opts for transformation driven by new customer intelligence is the change of roles. Under the new regime it is the *frontline staff* who take responsibility for gathering information about what's important to customers. Management's role changes to become less dictatorial and more supportive. The leadership role of management is to enable frontline staff to transform the organisation, through the generation, collation and interpretation of customer knowledge. Managers can help to ensure that the organisation takes action systematically and all directed to customer purpose, based on understanding what value looks like in the eye of the customer and having data to support it.

Investigating an organisation: the experience of staff

Reflections from a frontline staff member

The following story outlines the experiences of one frontline person who made the Journey to Customer Purpose. So successful was he in demonstrating his ability to understand the true needs of customers and to present powerful cases for change that he later took on a service management role at the age of 20.

> When I was first approached by my manager to join a 'Sense and Respond' investigation I wasn't sure what to expect, and I entered into the investigation not being greatly enthusiastic because I thought I knew what it was going to be about.
>
> When we started the investigation, however, things seemed a little different. One of the first things that hit me was when we looked at the mindset change and leadership skills required and didn't even start to analyse the data. The first week taught me a lot more than the second week, which was more about gathering data and representing it. However, the first week was about how you need to change the way you think, the way you think about how the system works before you can improve it. It also helped me to see how to represent the reality of a situation without past prejudice or without putting any emotion or spin onto things. This is how a lot of people tend to behave and it's the way we've been taught in organisations, to put a positive spin on negative results.
>
> I discovered a huge amount about how our organisation works and some insights about my own personal behaviour. Taking a look at the

organisation, things were a lot worse than we expected and we realised that deep down we had a lot of work to do. However, there was a mixed bag of responses from the people we talked to, anything from a total backing and open arms to a defensive position. I will say that it was the middle managers that had the most difficult time as these were the people who had always been told they are responsible for all situations and therefore felt they had the most to lose or change; they were stuck in the middle. To overcome this we simply persisted to have leadership conversations where we presented them with the customer intelligence data to show a picture of reality. Having seen the reality of the situation, however, there were a few that went back into their shells and would not listen; those were the difficult ones to crack but eventually we did get through to the people with persistence and understanding people's forms of resistance and how the data can help them in their own situations.

At the time I was nineteen years old and it was the simpler things, like being able to afford a car and being able to go out and buy a house that seemed important. So I was surprised to find myself, a frontline person, talking to senior management about ways for improvement – and they listened! I remember speaking to the Business Director and telling him ways of improving his business and talking about ways to save millions of pounds by altering the way we work and using customer data to make informed choices. I was a frontline person and I was speaking with the Business Director who is the head of the contract and manages about 450 people. There were five levels of management between him and me, but we presented him with a business case to change.

An example of one of the first things we addressed initially was a simple processing improvement where we had to transact with a third party to resolve incoming demand. The nature of the work was resetting customers' computer passwords; however, we had no control over the third party's computer systems. When we investigated the nature of this demand we found that the average customer experience was about one hour, but could vary from 30 minutes to 200 hours! Presenting the data to management informed them that from 2500–3000 calls every single month, we were wasting 2000 man-hours for the customers who were unable to work during that time. This created the business case for change. When we implemented the change to our process, training and job roles, we reduced this 'time to fix' to just 2 minutes. The management also told me that over the life of the contract we reduced the cost of processing this work by several million pounds. The reduction in this time had an even greater impact on the customers' customers, and these were people in society and in government – they had huge responsibilities. The ability to do the password resets within our area meant that our first-time-fix percentages increased by 60 per cent. Now the client's ability to deal with the public improved; they were able to deal with fifteen hundred more cases each month.

I go into meetings with clients now and I'm perfectly happy to be totally open with them and ask them if we've done something wrong. They were used to people lying to them and putting a positive spin on things or not presenting all the information. The reaction that I have had from the client since has been absolutely great, and customer satisfaction has increased. There is much more honesty and trust in the relationship.

PART III

The Journey to Customer Purpose: Re-Mind

Introduction

Bernard Marr
*Research Fellow, Cranfield School of Management;
and Visiting Professor of Organisational Performance,
University of Basilicata*

Today's business world is different from the business world even a decade or two ago. Currently, companies have to cope with increased complexity created by phenomena such as increasing customer demands, shorter product life cycles, global competition, and tighter integration of the value delivery chain.

The world has moved from a sellers' to a buyers' market. Especially after the two World Wars, markets in most of the developed countries were fuelled, demands outstripped supply, and suppliers controlled the market. However, global trade has gradually changed towards a buyers' market. Such markets are saturated and do not absorb all goods produced. Customers have improved access to information and knowledge through improved information technology, most notably the internet. In a buyers' market consumers hold the power, as they have a choice of what products or services to buy, and are better informed and more demanding. In such markets, differentiation and innovation become critical.

The increasing collaboration between firms means that companies' boundaries are becoming increasingly blurred. Customers are interested in solutions to their problems and value added. Organisations need to understand what these demands are, and what value means in the eyes of their customers as well as other stakeholders.

This shift in business context also means that many traditional cost-focused management tools do not provide managers with adequate or sufficient information. Many tools and approaches still in use in many organisations today were developed for suppliers' markets. Many of them are in fact quite Tayloristic. According to Frederick Winslow Taylor, it is only a matter of matching people to a task and then supervising, rewarding or punishing them in accordance with their performance. In Taylor's view, there is no such thing as skill and all work could be analysed step-by-step, as a series of unskilled operations that could then be combined into any kind of job. I believe that in a world where differentiation and innovation are critical drivers of success, we need new tools that help us to navigate in this new climate.

Companies need a clear understanding of their intangible assets and how these help to deliver the value proposition. They need to manage the competencies of the employees, the knowledge flows, the brand image, the relationships with stakeholders, the processes and routines, as well as the organisational culture. These are all components of the organisational resource infrastructure that enables companies to continuously innovate and differentiate.

In this book, the authors address many of today's management challenges by drawing together their experience gained from many years of working in business. What makes this book credible is that its ideas derive from real implementation success in companies, including the Japanese IT giant Fujitsu. This book will provide managers with a set of new perspectives, which is critical for today's challenging business environment. Managers will learn how to leverage their intangible resources in order to continually innovate and differentiate – activities that are the essential drivers for a sustainable competitive advantage.

CHAPTER 5

Re-Mind:
changing mental habits

Changing mindsets

Organisations need both a mind shift and a skill shift. As your aim is no less than transformation of your organisation, inevitably you will be working to change the mindset of all employees: executives, managers and staff. Most current management thinking stems from the mass-production paradigm. Revealing, challenging, and then replacing the old paradigm is what Re-Mind is all about.

This chapter lays out the theoretical rationale for creating an organisation capable of continually *sensing* the needs of customers and *responding* to these needs. The thought models conditioned by mass-production thinking are very powerful and pervasive, and re-engineering people's mental models is probably the most important aspect of organisational change – without a change in thinking, there can be no lasting change in practices: the organisation simply does business as usual, only better.

The type of change we are advocating strikes at the very heart of the organisational psyche, but the full adoption of the new principles will lead to the creation of an exceptional workforce: a workforce that thinks in a completely customer-focused way, adopting the new principles and producing products and services that fit customer purpose. It is a common misconception that to accomplish such a change you must change the whole infrastructure and go through a complete top-down re-engineering process. This is not the case: instead, by enabling the staff to be customer-focused, you enable a gradual, systematic realignment of the infrastructure to meet customer purpose, using customer intelligence data and end-to-end measurement as the yardsticks for change.

For organisations, the pressure to change is stronger than ever, yet in this complex world *making* changes is harder than ever. Our approach is to build an organisation with the right mindset to keep redesigning itself against the needs of the customer, not to have some theoretical managerial group meeting periodically to decide in some logical way how the business 'ought' to

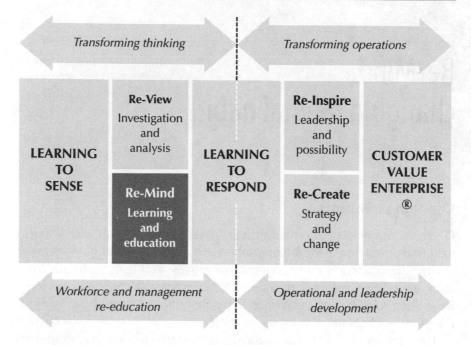

Figure 5.1 The Journey to Customer Purpose: Re-Mind

change and then creating a change programme to make this happen. The problem with this latter approach is that by the time the new ideas are implemented, the needs may have changed, and customers may require something other than what the organisation is now offering. We are not challenging the need to think logically; rather we are challenging the theory behind the logic (Womack and Jones, 1996), and in consequence the conclusions that flow from the logic.

Paradigms and customer intelligence

Even when 'adaptiveness' has come to be seen as a desirable quality, it cannot just be added on to an organisation's existing capabilities: the organisation *itself* must become adaptive.

Shifts in paradigms can happen in a number of ways: slowly, from one generation to another, such as the transition from a farming economy to an industrial one; dramatically, through some scientific discovery; or occasionally through an intuitive jump to a new perspective by one enlightened soul. It is also possible to seek new paradigms systematically, through the application of investigation and learning. In the world of business the need to search for new paradigms is often driven by the desire to create differentiation, to rejuvenate business or to seek out new markets.

Usually one of two common factors or both (Gharajedaghi, 1999) is at work when a paradigm shift occurs: either the creation of a new set of circumstances changes reality, or a change in the approach to learning and investigation yields new insights – or both together.

Beyond analytic techniques

Most analytical investigation techniques involve breaking things down into individual components and seeking to understand each component in turn, in the belief that understanding the components will yield insight into the whole. This approach has been very successful in exploring the world of physics and the physical world. However, it is not sufficient to understand the parts if the whole is greater than the sum of the parts.

> Take the properties of the elements hydrogen and oxygen. These are thoroughly understood in themselves. Yet nobody has ever succeeded in predicting the properties of water from a knowledge of its constituent elements. Trying to explain why water spirals down a plughole simply from a knowledge of atoms is an impossible task. What's missing is a knowledge of fluids – a whole level of order above that of individual atoms.
>
> Goodwin (1998)

Knowing your customers

Complete understanding of system dynamics, complexity and chaos still eludes us. However, new sciences, which look at emergent characteristics, are starting to throw light on some of the simple forces and laws that create complexity. In understanding organisations, too, the tools of mechanistic and reductionist thinking have proved insufficient: organisations are better examined using the science of systems, emergent properties and contextual dynamics (Gharajedaghi, 1999).

Today's competitive advantage is no longer about information, but about *customer intelligence* – the context in which customers operate provides insight into the value they seek. Information technology has created great storehouses of factual information, but contextual information is needed also if it is to be meaningful. It is as though some great fossil hunter gathered up all the specimens in the world and put them in one place to make examination more efficient; true, they are all together, but they have been separated from the very information that gave them meaning – the position they occupied in the strata, their proximity to other fossils, and details of the environment the fossilised creatures had lived and died in. The contextual information is missing, and the intelligence it could have yielded has been destroyed.

Businesses that can systematically capture and utilise customer intelligence (context) through flexible processes and insightful staff are blessed with a core competency that is difficult to reproduce on demand. In such organisations, customer intelligence can be quickly shared and acted upon, creating responsiveness and agility in aligning the organisation with market and customer needs.

The challenge for managers

So what does a shift of this nature feel like to managers? For a moment, imagine yourself at a conference or seminar. You know nobody at the event. During one presentation, the speaker asks everyone to take out their wallets or purses and asks you to hand yours over to the person sitting behind, and then turn to the front again. That person is asked to rearrange the contents in your purse or wallet and then to return the wallet to you.

What thoughts would go through your mind? What most people in that situation would fear is a loss of control; and soon some questions and doubts would arise: '*Will I get my wallet back? Will something be taken? Will he/she notice how disorganised my wallet is? What will he/she think about my personal items?*'

The feelings you have on being asked to do this are much the same as the feelings experienced by managers when asked to involve frontline staff in decision-making. They experience the same initial shock when asked to change their current command and control structures at work. They fear loss of control. They are unsure about the level of trust, self-doubting about their own capability, and – worst of all – afraid that something might be exposed that they have managed to keep hidden for some time.

Understanding the system

Our aim is to create a service organisation capable of responding on demand to customer needs. We therefore need first to consider how, using a customer-focused philosophy, we can design, build and operate this organisation, identifying the principles and theories that will foster the right conditions, behaviour and performance. We begin by identifying purpose-related measurements (Seddon, 1992), then examine how the end-to-end service performs today. These new understandings will provide the business case for change, and start the journey to responsiveness and organisational realignment with customers. This process will lead us naturally to a completely different 'on demand' culture.

Disconnections

Too often, employees are disconnected from the business imperatives. Measurements are disconnected from the work; workers are disconnected from customer purpose; managers are disconnected from customer value. Managers in these businesses are focused on functional goals, driving productivity, and increasing output. The system structures actually constrain the way people work and condition the way they behave. Often a dictated design, imposed from the top, creates an environment in which staff have little choice in the actions they take. Even when they see not only the problem but possible solutions to it, they are not allowed to respond creatively because the design has not catered to allow staff innovation.

If employees are focused on internal targets and metrics and are unable or not allowed to change the system in which they operate, two things can happen: *either* the staff will distort the data, *or* they will distort the system – or both. Either way, the information channelled up through the organisation to management bears little likeness to reality. Naturally, any changes that are introduced in response to misleading data may actually be, and often are, counter-productive. At its worst, misguided changes based on wrong data bring management into disrepute with the frontline staff, who often cannot understand why the managers have made these changes. Furthermore, they bring frontline staff into disrepute with the managers, who often cannot comprehend why their staff would distort the data, because they cannot realise that the system is conditioning the staff to do this.

Another common by-product of this situation is when frontline staff are focused solely on internal measurements, and are therefore processing work irrespective of its value to the customer. They may easily disengage their minds from serving the customer and instead end up serving the 'internal numbers'. This situation is what we call 'an assembly-line-of-the-mind syndrome' (Taylor and Bain, 1999).

Imagine for a moment that just *one* individual in your organisation is manipulating performance data and that *one* other person is subsequently taking action on the basis of that manipulated output. The very idea is alarming! Now roll out that possibility across *every department* within your organisation. Clearly senior management must not be allowed to make decisions based on manipulated data.

Organisational constraints

The system in any organisation comprises the policy, the role design, the reward and recognition systems, the processes and procedures, the performance measurements and targets, the technology, and so on (Figure 5.2). In

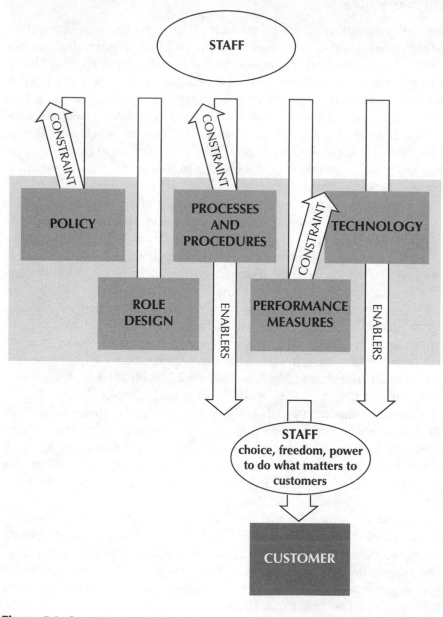

Figure 5.2 Organisational constraints

many organisations, the system characteristics intended to serve the business imperatives instead restrict choice, freedom and power to act (Gharajedaghi, 1999).

In order to design an organisation that meets customer purpose, identifying, understanding and quantifying the current constraints is very important. You will find it helpful to quiz your people on how they think your organisation should be designed and to understand their viewpoint. Get them to consider what they think is holding them back. If you ask customer-facing staff 'What is getting in your way? What could be improved?' you are likely to be presented with a vast array of innovations. However, you need to exercise caution at this point, as your staff will tend to suggest ways to change the things that currently get in the way of meeting *established* work routines and measurements. In effect, they will propose changes that will simply improve the usual approach.

Reacting to customer purpose

Customer purpose is in a constant state of change, so the organisation needs to be in a constant state of change to keep up.

The Theory-to-Performance Model demonstrates that the design, operational behaviour, culture and performance are actually emergent properties of the way people think. Applying Customer Value Principles allows the design to emerge in response to customer demand. Using this new approach, you actually know what you need to produce, and you can set up all the capability units to create it. You can then build and operate the system so that it produces what the customer wants.

Changing organisational thinking

Staff at all levels need to practise an entirely new way of thinking in order to implement a new way of working. This will be a huge institutional change, requiring the unlearning of attitudes and practices that previously had been accepted as both necessary and required by management. From such novel thinking, a new view of how to meet customer demand often emerges.

Denial and complacency

Some people will welcome this new approach: they may even recognise in it a freedom they were already craving. Others, though, will find it hard to change, and may deny that there is any need to do so. Here are some examples of the kind of language that indicates understandable resistance:

- 'We already meet customer demand.'
- 'We already have reports to say that our customers are happy.'
- 'We don't need to change the way we think.'
- 'We don't need to learn a different way.'
- 'We already have quality programmes focused on measurements, targets and the way our staff behave.'
- 'Who's going to pay to ensure that our organisation thinks in a different way and can learn something different?'
- 'How are you going to train everyone?'

In an organisation undergoing transformational change in search of customer purpose, such issues need to be addressed directly.

If frontline staff are in denial, they probably believe that everything is the responsibility of their managers: for them to change, their manager has to change things for them. An organisation that continues to do the things it has always done, with the same patterns of thought that it has always applied, will become lethargic and stagnant. Such an organisation is unlikely to be able to meet the changing needs of its customers, so the organisation will probably become extinct – at best, it is already endangered.

Staff are in denial because over the years they have developed a distorted view of what it means to meet customer needs. Many individuals perform in the organisation according to some significant past event, whether minor or major: that event dictates what they pay attention to at present. How they deal with the work that's coming in *now*, and what they pay attention to in terms of measurements, targets or standards, are both predicated on what went before. However, this is self-reinforcing: what they are paying attention to now will also drive their actions in the *future*. Experience shows that when events in the past dictate what happens in the present, and when this in turn is driving future actions, the present can easily become distorted and collapse into an unreal, misconceived view of reality.

In this world where people are afraid to act positively on the future because of events in the past, the organisation can become extremely internally focused. This type of organisation has '*blame storming*' as the norm. Rather than take responsibility and take action, people would rather stay and complain about how bad it is, justify why they *cannot* take action, and blame someone else for inaction.

It is very important to understand how powerfully the past can influence the future, and how it can actually stop people in their tracks. People may become fearful of failure or afraid of looking bad; they may be afraid to take responsibility; they may be afraid of stepping out and contributing ideas because they feel that their organisation has not listened in the past to their ideas and may not pay attention to them this time either. In reality, the organisation needs these people to be drivers for change.

What to measure in a Customer Value Enterprise®

Measuring demand

An organisation that can determine different demand types, can understand the new operating principles and has created the means to measure from end to end is moving towards customer-centricity. The organisation now needs to apply *purpose-related measurements*, because it now has a new way of looking at the way the work operates cross-functionally. It has to move away from the functional vertical measurements, which are all disparate, to a single common set of horizontal measurements that unify all the departments involved in the value chain.

The customer purpose defines value, and value defines meaningful work. The organisation and its leaders now know what to optimise, what to remove, what types of demand to increase, and what types of demand may present opportunities to create new products or services.

Consider Figure 5.3. The horizontal axis asks: 'Does it matter to customers?' The vertical axis asks: 'Is this a functional measurement or an end-to-end measurement?' The result is four categories. If you take each of your measurements and put it in one of these four categories, you may well find that some actually fit across two categories, as illustrated in the diagram. You may find that other measurements belong in the bottom quadrant, 'Functional' and 'No'. These measurements – 'average speed of handling', 'average time', 'first-time fixes', 'calls per person per day', 'sales per unit' and the like – are just functional and they really don't matter to the customer.

When implementing a Customer Value Enterprise® measurements should always be end-to-end, because it is the end-to-end performance of the whole organisation that actually creates value for the customer. The types of measurements needed are purpose-related, and for each one must ask: *does this matter to the customer?*

The answer is not always obvious, and the only way to get an accurate indication is by measuring end-to-end. Measurements such as 'total elapsed time' and 'capability to deliver value' are good examples. Others might be a first-time fix – does that matter to a customer? One answer is 'Of course it does!', but the organisation can also look more creatively at the question

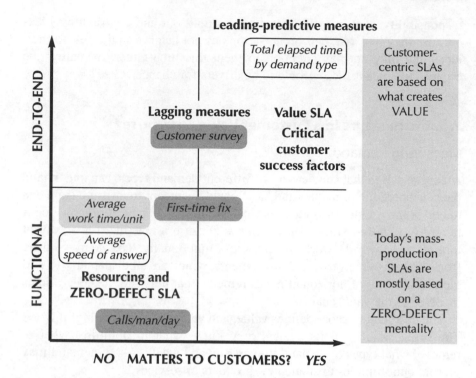

Figure 5.3 Understanding measurements

and ask, 'Why does the customer need to have the fix at all?' This is a perfect example of a measurement in need of complete removal: it serves no valid purpose in the new customer-centric world.

Setting value goals for staff

One presenting problem is that existing measurements like this, particularly in the service centre environment, are of no consequence to the customer and really do not matter to the employees: they are actually implemented to monitor resourcing. 'Numbers of calls per day' is a resource measurement, used because a business wants to get the maximum productivity out of its staff.

A common practice in service centres is to stipulate that if incoming demand is 'x', then each person in the centre needs to answer 'y' calls. But when turned into a target this becomes problematic, because it is completely outside the capability of the people in the service centre to improve the resource. They are incentivised only to make sure that the work gets processed in the allotted time. Little wonder, then, that work is actually passed on incomplete and without having created value. Incomplete work generates further units of work, but is not recognised for what it is: more waste being generated. Instead, it is seen as yet another unit of work to add to the already large number of units of work waiting to be processed. In the lean world this is known as *demand amplification*.

Measurements of this kind serve only to feed the efficiency trap, because when an organisation uses resource measurements as performance indicators for staff, it institutionalises the whole dynamic of locking in waste. This generates frustration for the customer and *prevents* frontline staff from creating value by improving the system and the service. Instead of adding value, staff learn to keep their heads down and get on with the job, putting their minds in neutral. Much better, then, to set the creation of value as the goal for staff. Staff at the frontline can then actually improve the end-to-end process by collecting and disseminating the right information, by looking at ways to eliminate the work entirely, and by improving the organisation's end-to-end capability.

To build a true Customer Value Enterprise®, you need to evaluate frontline staff by measuring not their *output* but the *outcomes* of their work, which often occur further down the value stream – sometimes much further. *Purpose-related measurement* actually achieves that. One problem with the conventional measuring system is that it makes comparisons between individuals based upon their individual outputs: if one person is taking 50 calls per day, it is 'normal' to expect any others who are taking fewer calls to increase their number to 50. This leads to the practice of 'buddying' or 'pairing up'. However, this does not take into consideration the *outcomes* of those calls, often way down the line in another function within the system. Regularly, it turns out on closer investigation that the person who takes *fewer* calls actually has *better* outcomes – because he or she creates more value.

Drawing comparisons on *outputs* and not *outcomes* usually increases both the costs to the organisation and the frustration for the end-user. Through buddying and pairing up, an organisation may transfer the skills needed to do the work successfully – but buddying and pairing up may also lead inadvertently to staff teaching each other techniques on how to beat the system.

Focusing on customer benefits

In the traditional arena, service-level agreements are usually based on a zero-defect mentality; service-centre measurements are based upon answering a certain number of calls on time; fast-food companies goal staff on not exceeding cost targets for waste food; and sales targets are based on signed orders. While these measurements are important, they are seldom within the control of the people who operate within the system.

These goals are heavily influenced by the 'capability' of the system. A systems capability is a matter of design – 90 per cent of all performance factors are *designed* in, not *managed* in (Edwards Deming, 1982). Any 'system' has a capability to produce certain outcomes: an organisation is no different.

Success should be based on specific outcomes such as these: 'Did this actually allow the customer to perform better?' 'Did this actually create customer success?' For many organisations this measurement is a step too far – many will be very wary and will consider this too difficult to achieve, not least because they fear that they might be requested to make recompense for some consequential loss. In reality, many customers are already making consequential losses and are amazed to get consequential gains!

Customer-centricity creates a company that is delivering customer success, rather than delivering only to a contract. Organisations that deliver to the contract only, and that do not look for anything over and beyond that contract, should not be surprised if customers defect to a competitor from which they receive added value. Defining customer success, turning that into the measurement system, and then driving all your capabilities to meet that measurement, actually creates success and longevity for the customer relationship and for the organisation. Traditional approaches focus on *outputs*: a Customer Value Enterprise® focuses on the *means to create output*.

Effectiveness is a dimension often left out of measuring systems. Most measurements are focused on production speed, efficiency and cost-cutting. What this new thinking creates is the advocacy of goods and products that create value for customers, meet customer purpose, and meet end-to-end effectiveness measurements – and all this, combined with efficiency measurements, create the most effective win–win situation.

Efficiency and effectiveness

Products and services must create customer successes, but an organisation still needs the capability to deliver them efficiently. Establishing a measuring system that satisfies both the organisation and the customer thus becomes a prerequisite to offering true value. This concept may seem like common sense, but it is not common practice. Organisations can become confused about resource measurements and performance measurements, and may confuse *efficiency measurements* with *effectiveness measurements*.

This often leads to chaos. Consider an example. While driving from London to Cardiff by car, you need to make the journey averaging 55 miles per gallon. That is an efficiency measurement, and you may manage to hit your fuel efficiency target. However, this efficiency measurement is totally irrelevant if you ought in fact to be driving to *Manchester*, which is in a completely different direction – you have measured your efficiency, but failed to measure your effectiveness.

It is understanding where your organisation actually *ought* to be going that is important. Consistently arriving at the right outcome, delivering effectively and being efficient at achieving it every time, creates customer success. An efficient flow creates a real value proposition for the customer and the organisation.

The real challenge is to identify what customers perceive as value and then to turn that into a measurement. When this measurement is in place it becomes possible to evaluate how the end-to-end processes create value at every single stage and at every single customer touch-point.

The old paradigm is that workers do and managers think. Because of this, the people who *do* the work are not usually the ones who *measure* the work. Under the new philosophy, however, those who perform the work are also the people who actually implement the purpose-related measurements, who measure what matters to the customer, and who evaluate their own performance against that. The task for managers is to create the capability and to remove the organisational constraints that hinder the frontline staff in delivering goods or services to customers.

CHAPTER 6

Re-Mind:
a new way of thinking

Moving towards Customer Value Principles

Building an organisation capable of sensing and responding can only be accomplished when those involved clearly understand the constraints created by the traditional philosophy and then realise that this philosophy does not serve the customer purpose.

Addressing 'wrong' thinking

Some employees and managers will grasp the Customer Value Principles quickly. Others will be sceptical or critical and will need to go through an experience that helps them understand how their current thinking is predicated by past events and by behaviour with which they are familiar.

What we term as 'wrong' thinking are comments such as these:

- 'Change is too big.'
- 'Change is too difficult.'
- 'Large-scale change begins at the top of the organisation.'
- 'The internal measurements are fine, so management and staff must be doing OK.'
- 'Staff are not intelligent and can perform only basic tasks.'
- 'Management must impose productivity targets and closely monitor staff.'
- 'Staff don't cheat in order to survive.'
- 'Individuals have control over their own performance.'
- 'The goal of the organisation is simply to make and sell.'
- 'The organisation is already customer-focused.'

Managers may receive information based on internal measurements that have been manipulated, stating that all staff are happy, or that staff do not cheat or manipulate the figures in order to survive in a world where they are driven by internal measurements. Such statements are serious examples of wrong thinking or systems failure.

Each individual can choose her or his own performance, and when to take action. When the system is wrong and when flow is restricted by processes, however, staff are disenfranchised, their roles are not empowered, and those choices simply do not exist.

Addressing ideas that block change

Imagine, then, that you have a new approach, you have new principles, and now you need to establish new thinking. But what happens about the *old* thinking? Old thinking can continue to get in the way. In fact, it can prove so ingrained as to be extremely counter-productive in moving the organisation forward, sometimes to the point of being totally obstructive. Old thinking can manifest itself in statements such as 'This scale of change should be driven from the top of the organisation.' Statements such as this one are an abdication of responsibility to take action.

On many occasions when the system is constrained, managers resort to the notion of 'empowerment' as if the *declaration* of empowerment will, of itself, allow staff to overcome constraints. In contrast, we believe that empowerment actually comes from the *design of the work*: it is not something that any one person gives, but a property of the system, there by design. In the more commonly accepted use of the word, therefore, one has to question whether empowerment really exists.

Another type of thinking that prevents change is the presumption that staff are not intelligent or skilled enough to create the type of organisation that managers wish it to become, or that they can only perform basic tasks under careful supervision. These views lead to the imposition of productivity targets and to close monitoring, with all of the resultant emergent properties that these create.

Such old thinking creates a negative spiral, highlighting its destructive power. A perfect example is how, if this old thinking is allowed to persist, the organisation as a whole may pay only lip-service to the implementation of change. As already discussed staff, through manipulation, will distort either the data or the system. Similarly, managers may think that individuals have control over their own performance: yet because what is deemed 'performance' is actually an emergent property of the way that somebody has built, designed and operated the organisation, it makes little sense to believe that individual performance can be down to an individual. Traditionally, staff have very little influence in the way the organisation performs.

Being skilled in the art of understanding how products and services create value for customers is the goal of applying Customer Value Principles to an organisation. Unlike traditional command-and-control organisations, this philosophy does not allow a business to seduce itself into thinking that it is already customer-focused just because it is meeting its targets and internal measurements. So how do we eradicate this old thinking – thinking based on experience that seldom comes up with new solutions? The solutions that have been experienced will serve only to solve yesterday's problems: simply business as usual, done better. To be truly customer-focused you need to address what happens today in response to external requirements, not to internal difficulties. This is not about rearranging the organisation's furniture: this is about rebuilding the house.

Operating principles for customer value

A Customer Value Enterprise® promotes the following principles:

- manage the organisation as one system, and understand it as one system
- capture and understand why the customer transacts
- measure the *value creation* to *value restoration* ratio
- deliver to customer purpose at every step of the value chain
- apply end-to-end measurements throughout the value chain
- implement purpose-related measurements
- create continuous flow by eradicating the batch-and-queue system that is prevalent in traditional organisations
- make those responsible for data input responsible for analysis also, and enable them to act on the data
- measure and reward your frontline staff on value creation
- measure and reward your managers on creating capability
- measure individual performance against customer success
- engage in the relentless elimination of corporate waste
- sense when customers are pulling service from your organisation and respond on demand.

The concept of empowering *roles* rather than *people* requires a fresh approach to existing management thinking. The redesign of the work flow is an enabler for such change. The benefit of having a skilled, knowledgeable workforce able to respond throughout the business where the skills are needed, is an unassailable differentiator, setting the organisation apart from its competitors.

Empowering frontline staff

By empowering the role of the frontline staff, you free staff from the constraints of the organisation, thereby enabling them to gather intelligence and have conversations – something that under the mass-production philosophy would have been seen as wasting time. The old way of thinking was that frontline staff were just there to get things done more quickly. In general business terms, no one ever talks of *management* being empowered, because empowerment is an expected part of their role: in a Customer Value Enterprise® the frontline staff are expected to show leadership and inter-departmental initiative as a matter of course.

Another important point about behaviour is not to trade opinions. Instead, collect the data relating to purpose, and understand how the organisation responds to that purpose. It is the frontline staff and the immediate frontline management who receive this information. It is *they* who are in a position to articulate, from a point of knowledge supported with data, what really needs to happen in the rest of the organisation to create the change in serving customers. To trade opinions without having collected the data is to invite mayhem; it opens the door to all the conflicts, the politics and the gaming. There is no place for this in an organisation that is sensing and responding and putting the customer at the very centre of all its actions.

Creating the flow of value

Let the work dictate the design

Creating flow is an important feature of an on-demand 'pull' service (Womack and Jones, 1996). The concept is simple, yet the practice can be difficult. Usually the current organisation is based on a batch-and-queue system, whereby work gets stockpiled and moved around departments. In manufacturing this can be seen in the form of inventory waiting in staging areas; in services it can be seen as sorting and prioritising service requests, tiered services such as 'first-line, second-line', sorting invoices into batches for processing, and so on. A simplified illustration of both approaches can be offered in the ways two fast-food chains have approached the task of preparing food and serving customers.

Most fast-food burger chains follow, to a large extent, the batch-and-queue principle. In one such chain each worker is assigned a particular task in the production and serving process. Food is cooked in batches, usually according to a forecast based on daily trends and the manager's intuition. The kitchen workers prepare ingredients to a forecast and wait for instructions to cook it. The food is then placed in a staging area for frontline staff to serve customers.

If the forecast is wrong, then either too much food is produced, resulting in waste, or not enough food is produced, resulting in lost revenue. Production in expectation of customer demand can result in high levels of waste, so staff in this situation are targeted on meeting demand and minimising waste.

The customer is offered a choice of standardised products and combinations. If the customer wants any other variety, then this can only be achieved as a special request – in effect, production by exception and priority. This circumvents the main production process, usually leaving this customer waiting much longer than other customers even though she or he is now getting special treatment. In this scenario, product standardisation reduces variety, thereby simplifying the production process.

Contrast this kind of flow with the one-piece flow achieved by another fast-food company that makes sandwiches and 'subs'. When you enter you are immediately offered a number of varieties of bread and rolls from which your meal will be constructed. You are invited to choose what ingredients you wish. You are free to look at the ingredients and to make choices based on what appeals. You give your order; and the ingredients you have chosen are placed in the sandwich, which is then passed to another worker who finalises the order and takes the money.

In this situation, the 'sandwich' flows as one piece, from the start of the operation to final completion. The customer is involved in every part of the process. Variety is built in and does not need special off-line treatment. There are no staging areas where food could go to waste: all food is produced *on demand*, not to forecast. All the workers are involved with the customer and with the creation of customer value. This enables workers to be involved in helping the organisation select new ingredients – they are closer to understanding particular customer needs. This allows the organisation to keep changing the variety offered, almost on a daily basis. Waste is minimal, because every order has a customer and is produced to her or his requirements. What has been standardised, therefore, is not the *product* but the *production method*.

Both approaches have been designed to solve a fast-food problem, yet the approaches are based on two quite different sets of principles. The mass-production approach – standardisation and the elimination of variety, functionalisation, batch-and-queue, and working to forecast – makes change difficult because the whole machine and the connecting procedures need modification and re-training. In contrast, the on-demand flow system, in which variety is designed-in, not designed-out, produces continuous flow. The customer is involved in the production process at every stage, and workers are engaged with the customer and can learn her or his likes and dislikes. Change is adaptive and daily.

From this simple illustration, it is evident that the second company is better placed to create variety on demand and to continually adapt to changing customer needs and even to local tastes. Both these companies are successful, but in a world where customers are demanding more variety, even successful organisations have to ask themselves, 'What do we need to do to maintain success? Are our current operating principles likely to cause us to lose competitive advantage?'

Let the customer define value

It is the customer, not the service organisation, who defines 'value'. If you can correctly identify customer purpose, you automatically know what 'value' is in the eyes of the customer. When you know what the *value* is, you can go on to identify the entire *value creation stream* that creates, contributes to and delivers that value.

Focus on every single step in the end-to-end process, ignoring all the traditional functions and boundaries. Identify and remove all the constraints to the flow. Anything that stops the work or holds it up – such as putting an item into a queue of work to be completed later – simply creates duplication: it increases costs and work, without increasing the *value* of the work. Remember: you are creating an 'on-demand' system. When it comes in, work needs to flow continuously: if it stops and starts, you don't yet have a truly on-demand service. One of the largest forms of corporate waste existing within most current businesses is speed without end-to-end continuity.

Very often the traditional organisation passes work from one department to another in a batch-and-queue system, and with this approach it is not atypical to discover that a task that could be done in ten minutes may actually take ten days to complete. The reason for this is simple: the process is *designed* that way. If you remove all the constraints to the flow, the work will move faster; you will avoid duplication; customers will get their goods or services noticeably quicker; and your organisation can now create value in a continuous flow on demand, without stoppages.

One cautionary note, however. Unless you take care to specify what value to the customer really is, the new processes you create will simply make *unwanted* goods or services flow faster. It's not enough that the *flow* is faster – if the goods and services you produce aren't of value to your customers, what you have is just sheer waste.

Engage staff in creating value

When researching and establishing how the value flows through the organisation and optimising value creation, you must engage the co-operation of the staff who do the work along that value chain. It is the *people* in your organisation who will create the transformational change and who will keep the value flowing. It is *their* understanding of what matters to the customer, *their* knowledge of the customer environment, and *their* knowledge of the way the system works that are fundamental to changing the way that the work flows and to building a better system.

Workers and departments organised on traditional principles have no need to talk to each other; they can just keep their heads down and keep working. However, this can lead to disengagement. You need to offer a different paradigm: one in which all staff feel confident and that their insights about the way in which work is done are important and valued by managers.

Managers need to carry out their operational analyses right where the action is: the customer-contact interface (Womack and Jones, 1996). It is by talking with frontline staff that managers will glean data with real value and come to understand the customer context. Working together in a cross-functional way actually joins up the company, as well as reinforcing and strengthening the value chain. The result is a critical mass of value creation around *flow* instead of around *functions*.

Effectiveness, not efficiency

The measurement of whether an organisation is producing the right services or products is a measurement of *effectiveness*, not efficiency. Once you comprehend *what is effective in creating value for the customer*, you are ready to start changing processes, products and services. Only when the right products and services are produced – when they are *effective* in delivering customer value – is the organisation ready to apply efficiency measurements. In the Customer Value Enterprise® world, effectiveness comes before efficiency.

When frontline staff have collected data from the customer perspective, few people within the organisation will have so strong a conviction to the contrary that they will *argue* with that data. The natural reaction from the staff is therefore to come up with innovative ideas to resolve any problems so that the organisation can deliver to the customer precisely what is being asked for. Frontline staff are free to experiment with ways to create value, so innovation becomes a way of life. Soon your organisation will become not only more flexible but also inherently innovative.

And what of your competitors? Some may feel inclined to mimic the innovations in your own organisation – but all they are copying is the service delivery. Unless they also undertake the necessary study of their own customers' needs, the service will eventually fail. Competitors who simply copy your 'solutions' will also have failed to address the thinking within their own organisations: if all they do is to graft customer-value innovations onto a mass-production methodology, the result will be further ineffectiveness and waste.

Keeping the organisation honest

Pretence, reality, and cost

'Pretence' in a business occurs when there is a gap between what an organisation *claims* to be doing and what it is *actually* doing. This pretence has an impact on staff, managers and customers. At all levels across the business, people need to establish the level of pretence that exists and to recognise both the emotional cost of that pretence to the individual and the financial cost to the business.

Organisations that have a large gap between the pretence and the reality will often find that their staff, in order to make the numbers, have either to manipulate the system or to manipulate the figures. In the worst cases, some staff may even feel compelled to lie about what they are doing in order to disguise the reality.

The personal cost to employees in organisations of operating in this way include:

- compromised honesty
- loss of integrity
- loss of freedom
- loss of enjoyment
- inability to have necessary conversations
- fear of being found out
- job-satisfaction eroded by being forced to focus on measurements unrelated to what really matters
- fearfulness about making changes.

The cost to the organisation is that its workforce no longer wishes to work in this environment: they have no integrity; they cannot take action; they have lost their creativity, innovation, choice, freedom, and power to achieve (Gharajedaghi, 1999). Predictably, an organisation such as this in which individuals feel disenfranchised will lose its staff.

How much pretence is occurring in *your* organisation? Lifting the lid on this will show you clearly what needs to be addressed.

But there's another side to this. Many organisations feel that they do not possess innovation, creativity and ingenuity when in fact they do. The problem is not that these attributes are missing, but that they are being applied uselessly in surviving the current system and its rules and regulations. This process – sticking to the letter of the law because that makes the numbers, rather than achieving the organisation's true purpose – is commonly known as 'gaming'. Instead of letting it be used to survive the current regime, it would be both more effective and more efficient for the organisation to harness this ingenuity in creating and experimenting with innovative ways to deliver service to customers.

What is needed is a new vision – a new view of reality. It is not enough to work merely on the basis of one's perceptions. The mistaken phrase 'perception is reality' is often offered to cover up things done poorly: if we can create a better perception, we don't need to worry that the reality hasn't changed. This is pure spin. The mantra when adopting Customer Value Principles is quite different: *perception is an opportunity to define what reality should be*. Instead of improving just the perception, let's make the effort to improve reality. In a Customer Leadership Culture, leaders cut though perception and get to grips with the reality. And for service organisations, reality is defined by the end-to-end organisational performance experienced by the customer.

The problem with any change is that some opinions may be deeply cherished, and may have been held for many years. If a person were suddenly to drop them, might not other people think worse of her or him? 'I might be thought stupid.' Or, 'My colleagues won't like me any more if I express different opinions.' A host of social stresses and face-saving activities pressure people back into old modes of thinking. It is simply easier to ignore reality and to live out a familiar pretence. Yet now that the pretence has been constructed, other people are making choices and decisions based on false premises.

There are real costs to this pretending (Table 6.1), for staff as well as for the organisation. Can managers set a lead in welcoming all staff to participate in a new possibility? Where a new beginning has been created, each individual can make a difference. If each person's insights and ideas are valued, each can help to turn the current pretence into reality.

Perceptions of customers – and customer perceptions

During the early stages of transformation, one thing that you will find is that the customer will perceive a small but important change. Staff will have slightly different conversations, and customers will feel that instead of coercing them through a process staff are engaging with them in a way that shows interest in and understanding of the customer's world.

Table 6.1 Pretence, reality and cost

PRETENCE *What we say it is like*	REALITY *What it is really like*	COST *What it costs us to pretend*
Caring for people	Attending to the	Low self-esteem
Giving people	numbers	Feeling of betrayal
opportunities	Just ticking the box	Lack of fulfilment
Coping; everything	Just fixing the problem	Withdrawing
is OK	Problem-orientated	Leaving; low morale
Doing a good job	Out of control	Loss of integrity
Working as a team	In denial	Loss of honesty
Listening to people	Having individual	Lack of fun
	agendas	Customer dissatisfaction
	Back-stabbing	Loss of repeat business
	Selfish	Cynicism
	Failing	Frustration
	Covering up	Feeling bad
	Lying	Cheating
	Mistrusting	Nothing gets better
	Blaming	Missed opportunities
	Cheating	A sense of futility

What really matters, though, is what's going on inside the organisation *in response to* these conversations. Are new decisions and new choices being made about what service or products will be provided? Are staff learning what aspects of their process need to be improved? Have staff started acting on the organisation on behalf of the customer?

Staff become the voice of the customer *within* the organisation. They provide the customer understanding and the true customer purpose. This provides the organisation's learning and opens up its ability to sense and respond.

Slowly at first, but increasing exponentially later on, things start to change. The organisation's concept of customer value starts to change. In response, the reward and recognition starts to change; processes start to change; the product and services start to change. At a certain point, when you have reached a critical mass within the organisation, change becomes very rapid. There is a lag between staff realising what matters to customers, staff recognising the constraints within the organisation, and staff then dismantling those constraints.

Seeing reality leads to transformation

Past practices must be placed firmly in the past, and employees must understand how this past is adversely affecting the workforce today. When the organisation is conscious of that and can actually put it to one side, a clear view of reality emerges. Seeing clearly for the first time, with the view no longer obstructed by previous solutions, staff will begin to see new solutions – things that have never been tried before. And as these solutions are tried, you will start to see their effect on customers.

Once you get data from the customer's viewpoint, the possibilities for change can suddenly become endless.

A change in thinking is achieved through coaching: coaching is one of the best ways to turn people into leaders who can then set about changing the corporate culture. Creating motivation to change is easiest when people are grounded in reality and understand data from the customer perspective and are willing to try to influence people around them. You don't need to manipulate them or to try to persuade them to do something: you can simply discuss the reality of the situation to them and ask for their assistance. Staff become engaged, and although some may still choose not to help, even they may feel inspired by the drive, the data and the energy shown by the Transformational Leaders. Word of mouth spreads quickly. One person may tell someone else that 'The customer service department' – for instance – 'has some really neat data and is trying to make some real changes. It sounds really interesting ... I wish *we* could do something like that. Why doesn't our department meet with them and discuss what they're doing?' It is the leader who starts attracting like-minded people. Followers seek out the leaders.

Our own understanding of the process of personal change has been informed by the workshops of Landmark Education. For transformation to take place within an *organisation*, individuals who have a new view of reality must communicate that new view to others. They need to spread that view into every part of the organisation, so that everyone, whatever their pre-existing beliefs and expectations, is touched, moved and inspired. Do you want your organisation to embark on a journey to customer purpose? Then you need first to address the thinking within your organisation. To paint the future, start with a blank canvas. Set aside preconceived ideas and established methods; set aside old solutions to old problems.

The organisation is guilty of thinking in the past when its employees say things like this:

- 'I tried that before: it didn't work.'
- 'Been there, done that.'

- 'If I do that, I'll get into trouble.'
- 'Just keep your head down.'
- 'Just do what you're told.'

Transformational Leaders need to establish what is really going on, not just what they *perceive* is happening. They don't get sidetracked worrying about how the reality became reality; they concentrate instead on how the organisation is going to get to the future.

To be able to move into the future as a Customer Value Enterprise®, it is crucial to identify where people are distorting the system or the data. There's a reason why this is happening, whether it's poor training, peer pressure, fear of consequences, or fear that mistakes or misrepresentations in the past may be uncovered. Note also that distortion of this sort does not indicate that staff are bad or dishonest people – it is merely that, within the constraints of the system, many have found a way to secure their jobs: they have followed the actions of colleagues in order to meet the targets and hit the numbers.

People may reasonably feel exposed or threatened, and yet an organisation cannot hope to move forward unless it first knows how things really stand. An organisation must want its staff to face up to reality and to stop pretending. These questions remain: 'What can an organisation do to make others feel safe about coming clean? What incentives can it offer to help staff disclose mistakes and misrepresentations?'

Unlearning the past, responding into the future

An organisation will have a new view of reality, because it is truly open to what reality might be. Frontline staff will be able to create new relationships with their customers, and to gather new information, customer knowledge and customer intelligence by having conversations with customers. The organisation will be able to determine the structure that is supporting and enabling the frontline staff, and to evaluate whether or not they are creating value for the customer.

The old way of thinking saw managers spending much of their time trying to control and drive the corporation, only to find out later that in reality they had very little control over change, or influence on it, unless they first altered people's thinking. The new approach creates leaders who are not conventional but free-thinking and who enable others, including frontline staff, to share leadership.

Consider these questions:

- Are staff within your organisation required to meet numbers in order to survive the measuring system?
- Is your organisation doing well because the measurements say so? If so, can they be trusted?
- How much control do individuals really have over their own performance?
- Are your customers as happy as customer satisfaction surveys show?
- In order to create this scale of change, must the decision come from the top of your organisation?
- How could you break down the walls of your organisation if those in power are in denial?
- In your organisation, who needs to unlearn what?
- If you establish a new reality, might you lose control?
- Will you like the view of reality?

Living through the change: the experiences of staff

Reflections from a frontline staff member

Here are the reflections of one frontline person who had been through the diagnosis of the working environment and had come to several realisations:

> I learnt that the service was not designed to give the customer what they needed, and there was a lot of apathy and frustration amongst all of us regarding the way we worked. This was my first job after leaving college; I had a very positive attitude when I joined. Then after a short period you learn that you just sit in front of a computer for eight or nine hours, just churning through forms, not really getting an understanding of why you're doing it. I started to feel desperate and asked myself, 'What is the purpose of this? What's the point and why am I here?' Now, having been through the analysis activities, I was motivated to work on improving things. The strange thing is that the findings seemed so obvious, yet no one had done anything about it for years – they were never confronted with reality, so it was a huge shock for many people. We discovered that we were just churning work, and people in middle management positions felt they had little control or power over what they were doing. The pressures of the system made them give artificial figures and behave in a way they would not normally. Things were a mess. Presenting our discoveries with the data and costs had a massive impact on everyone. I did realise, however, that my previous behaviour had been contributing to the situation.

Reflections from a manager

A manager who runs a customer account recalls her personal story of transformation when she viewed the organisation from a new perspective:

I became involved with the transformational work when I noticed other operations displaying strange information on their notice boards. It was customer data and it looked refreshing. When I inherited an account in need of attention, I knew a customer diagnosis and transformation was the right thing to do; however, I did have personal doubts as to whether I would be able to do it.

I had a number of presenting issues to deal with in my operation, including unpredictable customer demand and limited resources to respond. Staff attrition was very high at a rate of 50–60 per cent because the pressures of the environment were horrendous.

Customer satisfaction was at an all-time low and we were struggling to meet our contractual commitments. Staff didn't really understand what their roles were. I remember sitting next to people transacting with customers and I was shocked at how hard it was for them to do their job. When I asked questions like 'Why did you do that for the customer?' the response I got back was 'We are following the working instructions.'

So the investigation began and I got involved with the diagnostic team. My own team were not prepared to go through the investigation unless I invested my time and was committed in the same way they were. If I'm honest I did find it quite uncomfortable because it forced me to confront some issues around the way that I had been managing in the past and that I'd been making decisions on behalf of the operation but I didn't really understand how it worked end-to-end. I felt initially that I didn't have a contribution to make: however, when we captured the information about what's important to customers, we realised that we had rationalised data to present a positive spin. We began to capture more information about practices that were unreliable and out of date. When we started looking at some of the processes I realised I could no longer tolerate the mediocrity, waste, employee and customer frustration, and declared 'We are not going to do it like this any more.'

One of the biggest things I learnt was the huge potential in our people; I was completely overwhelmed by their enthusiasm, by their commitment, their determination to change things. They really seized the day; they saw this as an opportunity to change what they had inherently known was wrong for a long time. I was also incredibly impressed at how articulate they were in presenting to our clients, and the level of passion they conveyed about improving the business from the customer's perspective. Having managed service operations for ten years I had never seen anything like it. I was justly impressed. Very quickly operational performance started to improve, as did our relationships with the client. The senior management teams wanted to use our intelligence about their business to help formulate development plans. Our customer satisfaction rating increased from 2 out of 10 to 7 out of 10 over a nine-month period, and the remedial service demand reduced by around 45 per cent, and operating costs reduced by 26 per cent, in the same period.

We moved more skills to the frontline and gave people greater access to knowledge databases. We had hard and fast data to take away all of the previous objections of both senior management and client management teams – the ones who were stopping the operational changes.

The impact for me at a personal level was enormous and it has really improved my confidence. It has completely transformed the way I think about my work and made me realise I am capable of much more. I really believe that if I had not gone through such an intense process and experienced all the range of emotions I wouldn't have raised my work profile within the organisation, which isn't really something that I was actively seeking but just happens to be a natural outcome.

PART IV

The Journey to Customer Purpose: Re-Inspire

Introduction

Professor William Carney
Professor of International Marketing, Instituto de Empresa, Madrid; formerly Visiting Assistant Professor at George Washington University, Washington, DC

In a world where economic and technological expansion is driving trade and commerce towards one economic system, organisations have not only to rethink their business models but also to rethink their approaches to customers and differentiation.

Driving critical mass and volume are outmoded strategies for growth; only by the creation of differentiation through the insights and creativity of the entire organisation can businesses hope to stay alive.

In order to survive, nothing less than the engagement of the whole organisation with the process of understanding and responding to customers is required. This raises two issues. One, how do organisations encourage, capture and utilise the creativity of their staff? And secondly, how do they create business models that can rapidly change in response to a world where discontinuous change is prevalent?

Leaders at all levels need to embrace the type of entrepreneurship that is usually the preserve of the small business. Market drivers are now creating businesses capable of seeking out the real needs of customers and rapidly bringing to market differentiated approaches.

This calls for a shift in power – from command-and-control structures to providing frameworks for rapid prototyping and experimentation.

During the course of my research, one issue became blindingly clear, and that was that while much had been written about the importance of customer focus and the potential impact upon profitability, very few approaches existed that would actually allow an organisation to capture customers' problems and desires and subsequently to turn that input into products or services that delivered value to customers.

While simple in concept, the capability to become customer-focused often implied a change in company mindset as well as activities and processes that many organisations were loath to embrace.

Most, if not all, managers believe that customers really drive their business, and most believe that they cannot exploit many of the opportunities that present themselves because of the lack of organisational flexibility.

The concepts outlined in *Sense and Respond: the Journey to Customer Purpose* demonstrate alternatives to operating organisations. Leaders and managers need to rethink their roles and to view employees and customers from a new angle. Nothing less will do in a world where economic power and markets are constantly shifting.

CHAPTER 7

Re-Inspire:
the nature of leadership

Creating a Customer Leadership Culture

We can't solve problems by using the same kind of thinking we used when we created them.

Albert Einstein (1879–1955)

A Customer Value Enterprise® requires a new form of leadership which creates transformation and reinvention: leadership that challenges conventional perspectives and decision-making patterns, identifies barriers to change, recognises and breaks through functional and organisational conflicts, and provides intrinsic motivation that creates possibilities for others to succeed in a way that gives them choice, freedom and the power to do what matters.

To develop such leadership, management must enable the capacity to lead from all levels within the organisation, so that the organisation can profit from the human intelligence of all its staff. Resistance to change can be strong, and time is needed to create a new ethos. To create an entire leadership culture that will continually challenge assumptions, break through mindsets and transform thinking, one must start with individuals at a personal level.

Sharing responsibility

This new form of leadership may not come naturally. It challenges the traditional view that it is the responsibility of management alone to do the thinking and design the work practices. It addresses difficult questions of business integrity, alignment to customer purpose, and who is responsible for providing a view of reality. The new principles we advocate entail the creation of leadership roles at all levels, particularly at the frontline.

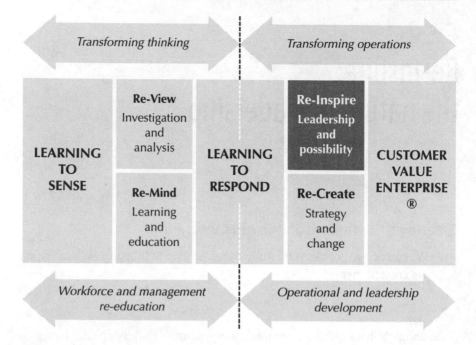

Figure 7.1 The Journey to Customer Purpose: Re-Inspire

Shifting responsibility for capturing the customer intelligence away from management and giving it to frontline operations is probably the biggest challenge for organisations. Attention to customer intelligence captured by frontline staff will transcend the hierarchy, operational structures, business process and governance. Frontline staff with this intelligence begin to align the organisation with real customer needs. Organisations can give frontline people the means to step into leadership and start to change relationships with customers, managers and colleagues.

It isn't always easy for managers to let go of control, and it isn't always easy for frontline staff to embrace the new freedom to lead. Challenging mindsets and structures is the toughest part of creating a new Customer Leadership Culture but the most significant. It is this shift of responsibility and power to the frontline that develops an organisation which is capable of continually locking onto the needs of customers and delivering sustained change. The new leaders create the means for transformational change within the organisation; the staff create the capability to sense and respond.

Engaging others

In their book *The Heart of Change* (2002), John P. Kotter and Dan S. Cohen talk about the reasons why people in organisations change:

> People change what they do less because they are given analysis that shifts their *thinking* than because they are *shown* the truth that influenced their *feelings*.

Kotter and Cohen assert that the heart of change is in the emotions, and that one can therefore catalyse

> action by *showing* people potent reasons for change that spark their emotions.

We go further: we say that to evoke change it is necessary to address the way people think and behave in response to how they feel. Not only does the organisation need to go back to basics in terms of the way its system is designed and the principles and theory of management under which it is established: it also needs to uncover the reality of why staff behave the way they do, what matters to them, how can they make a difference, how they can break free of institutionalised constraints, what are the origins of their behaviour, and what impact this has on day-to-day operations experienced by the customer.

Leadership: the art of the possible in the face of reality

A Customer Leadership Culture starts with individuals and at a personal level – individuals who generate new levels of performance and effectiveness. Transformational Leaders are not focused merely on improving what already exists: they are also willing to examine and challenge fundamental assumptions which shape people's actions and what they consider to be possible. Informed by customer intelligence data, they will confront the traditional boundaries of thinking, measurement and operating practice.

The performance of any organisation is the outcome of the collective interactions between staff, departments and customers. Organisational performance is in part a function of how well individuals perform within it, and their ability to do so depends on whether the organisation allows them to perform well. Do they have the *choice* to make decisions? Do they have the *freedom* to act? Do they have the *power* to do what instinctively they know matters? (Gharajedaghi, 1999.)

It is the fundamental way in which organisations have been designed that creates the constraints that inhibit change. These barriers exist throughout the organisation – in the technology staff use, in the policies they must follow, in the targets they must meet, even in the boundaries of responsibility created by their roles.

Barriers to change: organisational constraints

Once you understand that the way individuals behave within an organisation is a direct result of the constraints operating on them, you can start to take meaningful action. However, these barriers and constraints are often hidden from view and have been constructed for perfectly good reasons, often related to control, governance and tradition – 'That's just how things get done around here, and that's how it will stay.'

What will it take to challenge an existing operational design and capability when the organisation is reported to be 'doing okay' and delivering the numbers – even though frontline staff say that the operational design creates an environment in which people have no autonomy to address the changing needs of customers and their support infrastructures?

Barriers to change: staff resistance

The impact of the past

Ultimately, the way people behave and what they pay attention to will influence the success of the organisation. However, introducing a new way of operating can create behaviour that may be seen as resistance to change. This resistance occurs for lots of loyal and plausible reasons, which staff can defend quite convincingly by appealing to the organisation's history. At an organisational level, people have socialised their current thinking into their working practices: it has become normal and comfortable to go on acting and behaving in the way they did previously, which experience may have shown to be a way that did not attract unfavourable attention or create career-limiting situations.

Resistance to change takes many forms and differs from one person to the next. In many cases a person's inability to change is seen by colleagues as stubbornness or laziness. Some are placed on a 'performance improvement plan'; others are managed out of the business. The organisation, however, has failed to address the reasons why resistance has been created and how resistance came to manifest itself in the first place.

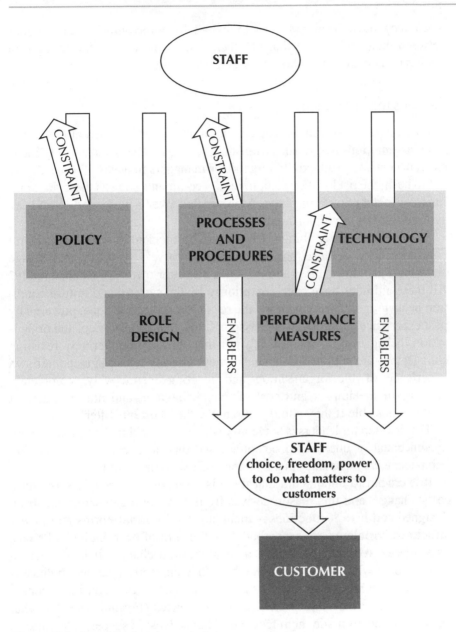

Figure 7.2 Organisational constraints

For some people, a problem can feel so real, suffocating and challenging that it seems impossible to break through it. For some these feelings have been created by past experiences – perhaps occasions when staff have tried something and failed, when they have done something and felt misplaced, or when they have been made to look bad by unfavourable comparisons between their ability and that of others. For some others, the thought of talking to their manager about changing something isn't easy.

Reasons for resistance

Careful attention to what people say in organisations will reveal the underlying assumptions and norms. Staff may say 'The managers are only interested in cost and productivity targets', or managers may say 'We've always got to be on the backs of our employees' – comments such as these are opinions and perceptions that have been created over a long period and are symptomatic of the organisational design.

'We tried to change things before and got knocked down for it'; 'Don't confront reality, because that's not seen as positive'; 'Don't try and change anything – just do business as usual but a bit better'; 'It's not that bad really.' All these attitudes have been conditioned by the system, and in turn condition behaviour and thinking now: the result is a protective zone, powered by past experiences, prejudices and assumptions, that simply keeps the organisation locked in its own past. It's not that staff are deliberately resisting change: they are simply doing what comes naturally to them given their own experience of the organisation and reacting instinctively, completely unaware of the impact and cost of their behaviour, and not seeing what could be possible if they could just remove their current 'filter'.

The first step for leaders is to identify what factors within the business cause dysfunctional or unexpected outcomes, and then to address the underlying behavioural characteristics that underpin the maintenance of those factors.

It is crucial to understand that there is a *reason* why people sometimes resist change, and this reason derives from how the organisation has been designed and how it functions – including the informal norms and power structures. Problems are exacerbated by the sum of each individual's past experiences, which have shaped their attitude to change. It is a shock to some people when they realise that how they currently react and behave is not a direct consequence of what actually happened to them, but a consequence of how they *interpreted* their experiences (Fromm, 1950) – what these experiences made them feel about themselves: 'a success', 'a failure', 'stupid', 'can't communicate', 'insecure', 'not liked', and so on.

Reducing interference

Remember: the conversations people have and the language they use will indicate what people are resisting or what stops them moving forward. It's a very simple way to discover what staff are feeling about the system: just listen to them. Listen within your own organisation, and notice whether you recognise any of the behaviour traits in the following section.

Myles Downey, in his book *Effective Coaching* (1999), talks about resistance to change and personal performance, and gives this equation:

Potential *minus* Interference *equals* [Personal] Performance.

The role of leadership is therefore to uncover the 'interference' and then to reduce or eliminate the causes. Downey's examples of interference or resistance can be seen in many circumstances. He suggests that the following are some of the most familiar:

- fear (of losing, or winning, or of making a fool of yourself)
- lack of self-confidence
- trying too hard
- trying for perfection
- trying to impress
- anger and frustration.

Examples of interference or resistance can also be heard as people listen to one another. Have you ever been misunderstood or failed to communicate something? Here, again from Downey, are some possible reasons why you may not truly hear someone else:

- other people talking
- what I thought they were going to say
- what I thought I should say
- they were boring
- I had already worked out what they should do
- I had already thought of what they were saying
- thinking of the next question
- thinking of my response.

All of this interference keeps us at a distance and stops us from getting into other people's worlds and understanding what's really important to them, including what will make a difference to customers. How can you discover this if all this noise is going on in your mind and you have another internal target to meet?

Probably the most common kinds of interference or resistance show up with teams of people who share no common purpose. Downey gives these examples of destructive team behaviours, some of which you may notice in your own organisation:

- lack of trust in other team members
- fear of ridicule
- pursuit of personal agendas
- hidden agendas
- rivalries
- fixed beliefs and positions ('This is how things are').

In contrast, true Customer Leadership Cultures have teams that show some of the following *constructive* team behaviours:

- an absence of hierarchy in relationships
- challenging conversations
- the pursuit of inspirational goals
- creativity, imagination and intuition as part of everyone's toolkit
- mutual accountability for the achievement of goals
- creating a 'pastless future' of possibility.

Choosing to change: frontline staff

A Customer Leadership Culture is not based on hierarchical position power; rather it calls for leadership at all levels of the organisation, including (and especially) at the frontline. We are not talking about leaders who need to be charismatic or to look good: we are talking about ordinary people who, because they pay attention to customers and gather customer intelligence data, can inform and create new possible ways of working which break through the barriers of fixed beliefs and structures. These people offer real leadership and bring about real change.

Fixed beliefs and structures compound the resistance to change; they are a key reason why people stay stuck in the past. During our work we tell the story of an old man sitting in his rocking chair on his veranda, in the sun, with his old dog lying next to him. The dog is groaning and moaning and gives an occasional howl. The man's neighbour comes to visit, to ask why the dog is making so much noise. The man explains that his dog is lying on a rusty nail; although it's clearly uncomfortable, the nail isn't painful enough for the dog to move. So it is with people: we may even be aware of our resistance to change and still convince ourselves that 'It's not that bad' so that we don't have to do anything about it. If we do that, we stay stuck where we are.

Louise L. Hay, in her book *You Can Heal Your Life* (1984), discusses the 'decision to change':

> Throwing up our hands in horror at what we may call the mess of our lives and just giving up are the ways many people react at this point. Others get angry at themselves or at life and also give up. By giving up, I mean deciding 'It's all hopeless and impossible to make any changes, so why try?' The rest goes, 'Just stay the way you are. At least you know how to handle that pain. You don't like it, but it's familiar, and you hope it won't get any worse.'

She goes on to describe that being aware of your own reality is only the first step:

> When we have a pattern deeply ingrained in us, we must become aware of it in order to heal the condition.

It is crucial for organisations to notice constraints and that staff are often trying to work within them, rather than addressing the reasons why the constraints exist.

Faced with proposals for change, some staff may object and claim that change is impossible (Fromm, 1950). Eventually they rationalise away their own freedom and every ounce of possibility that change might happen. We have already described how 'pretence' can become established in an organisation: as you listen to a litany of sincerely held convictions that change is impossible, you start to see the dramatic impacts and costs, to individuals and to the organisation, of this departure from reality.

The difficulty with any change is that some convictions may have been cherished for many years, and have come to underpin the very work that people are doing. Suddenly to dismiss them can cause deep-seated resentment or distress. Initial fear and resistance to change is often a reaction to the new reality: to different convictions. Staff may view change as undermining their work, their intelligence, their role or their standing in the organisation. Some may feel that it would appear hypocritical to change their viewpoint after holding contrary views for years. It is simply easier to close their eyes to the new reality and to continue to live out the previous pretence than to change their own mental habits and drive forward the new philosophy.

One of the comments that we often hear, particularly from frontline staff, is this: 'Well, it's all well and good you asking me to do things differently, but my manager won't let me.' That quite understandable mindset may be rooted in real experiences, and you can best challenge that history simply by

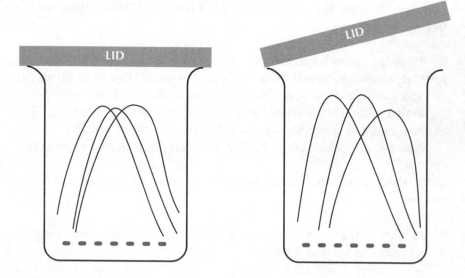

Figure 7.3 Training fleas

letting each individual live with the realisation of the impact and costs of her or his own mindset until eventually they begin to challenge themselves. Then give staff the data and allow them to talk to managers. They will discover that their opinion of the managers is inauthentic: that in fact the managers want the same things, but are themselves under different pressures.

We offer a simple illustration of how some sincerely-held convictions are products of their own pasts or of traditional organisational behaviour, or both – that they are indeed habits of mind which lead to pre-judgements rather than openness. Here's a story about how to train fleas, which may already be familiar.

The behaviour of fleas was observed, including how they reacted when they were put in a jar. At first all the fleas simply jumped out of the jar. When a lid was placed on top, they still tried to jump out. They soon discovered, however, that this was painful – every time they tried to jump out, they hit their heads on the lid. After a while, the fleas learnt to jump just below the lid so as to avoid their painful experience (Figure 7.3).

After a short while, when the lid was removed the fleas remained in the jar – they had conditioned themselves to such an extent that they could no longer see the opportunity when the lid was off (Figure 7.3). They were basing their future expectations of 'fleadom' on their painful experiences in the past. Even with the lid off, they remained in the jar and eventually died.

Individuals within an organisation and the colleagues with whom they associate define who they are when at work and how they behave. Familiarity is safe and secure: they know they will be able to handle whatever the job presents. There is an inherent need to survive. People may even stay in situations they find completely uncomfortable simply to justify an opinion of somebody else: 'You always do this to me, so I'm going to stay and be miserable, just to prove to you and to others that it's *your* fault.'

Similarly, employees may feel justified in not presenting new data to managers because their preconceived views about their managers' likely response seem more powerful than the new reality. This is often because the employees are at ease with their surroundings, even when those surroundings are not very comfortable. Why do people choose to stay in 'comfort zones' that – to an onlooker – seem uncomfortable? Often it is because they have become familiar with all the emotional elements contained in the situation: whatever happens, they trust they will be able to handle it.

So some people remain in situations that are uncomfortable but familiar, and they do so because of deep-seated convictions based on past behaviours. This creates what we refer to as 'discomfort zones'. And the biggest single reason why some individuals remain in their personal discomfort zones is this: *doing so absolves them of responsibility*. In their familiar setting, doing things the way they were shown, they genuinely feel that they are working responsibly.

Choosing to change: managers

Managers too are sometimes reluctant to change or to try new ideas, perhaps because they are comfortable with the situation as it exists, with all the hierarchical powers and reporting lines clear and defined. If they are required to move out of *their* comfort zone, they may feel that their power is being eroded or that the lines are being blurred.

Some are fearful, as described above, yet when the common purpose is defined they can begin to make informed choices and start to work outside their comfort zones. Managers can start to take on a new view of reality – to see something they couldn't see before, and to do something that wasn't possible before.

Getting in touch with reality

Rosamund Stone Zander and Benjamin Zander, in their book *The Art of Possibility* (2000), comment that blocks which we perceive to be external, and thus outside our control, may actually be internal, and thus open to change:

> Many of the circumstances that seem to block us in our daily lives may appear to do so based on a framework of assumptions we carry with us. Draw a different frame around the same set of circumstances and new pathways come into view.

Our perceptions of what is possible reflect our own assumptions and beliefs, and these may not even be conscious:

> All the manifestations in the world of measurement – the winning and losing, the gaining of acceptance and the threatened rejection, the raised hopes and the dash into despair – all are based on a single assumption is that life is about staying alive and making it through – surviving in a world of scarcity and peril.

If an organisation is to change, leaders need to dismantle these thought patterns, resistance, and the constraints from the organisational design.

We have found it helpful to introduce the concept of an *authenticity gap* (Figure 7.4), which is an indication of the difference between the pretence

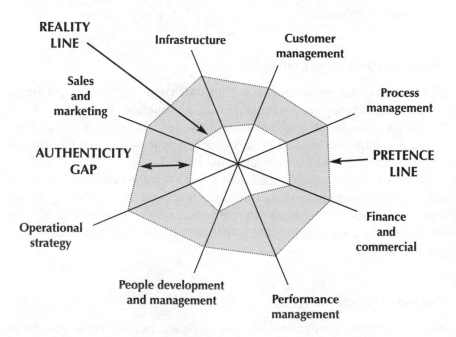

Figure 7.4 Authenticity gap

and the reality. For example, a company might claim to potential customers that it provides opportunities for its staff to develop, that it understands the true needs of its customers, that it designs the right technology solutions, and that it has the right processes and procedures. What company wouldn't? Yet were the customers to look at what really goes on in practice, and were they to ask the employees who work within the organisation to describe their real experience, a rather different picture might well emerge.

It isn't always easy to face reality and some organisational structures and policies may make it hard for employees to see reality: 'Yes – that happens … but it's not that bad, really? And anyway, we all pull together and work it out, don't we?' This type of reaction keeps people in a state of denial, a state in which they can become resigned and complacent about what's happening around them, a state in which they would rather suffer and rationalise the way it is rather than do anything to change.

For some, however, the new view of reality is a shock, but a welcome one. They find the business case for change compelling, and they form a clear picture of the work – and the *scale* of the work. The larger the authenticity gap, the greater the change that is required.

Transformational Leaders are no longer prepared to accept the costs of doing nothing, neither the costs to the customer nor the costs to themselves. They begin to gather customer intelligence data and to build a business case for change. As they transform their own thinking and behaviour, the organisation itself begins its transformational journey.

CHAPTER 8

Re-Inspire:
leading transformation

Customer leadership

As previously described, a Customer Leadership Culture recognises and defines what reality is for others. Leadership entails helping others to see a more accurate and insightful view, without preconceptions. To accomplish this, the leader must focus on revealing patterns of behaviour, the impact and cost of fixed beliefs and practices, the pretence, and the barriers and constraints imposed by the organisational design and structure. The new breed of leaders challenge existing mental models, foster strategic thinking, and provide a view of the interrelationships between people, departments and the customer. They bring customer intelligence data to conversations to provide a clear view of reality, and point out ways to make informed decisions and to take meaningful action. This range of skills, collectively called a *leadership spectrum*, is illustrated in Figure 8.1.

With their new view of reality, leaders are well placed to determine the state of the organisation and exactly what areas need to be addressed. Does the organisation offer a traditional environment, as shown on the left of Figure 8.1? Or is it on the right, already striving to create a Customer Value Enterprise®? Neither state is right nor wrong: what is important is that leaders reveal the *true* current state. Until you understand the foundation of your transformational journey, you cannot really determine what you want to create. Without this 'reality' starting point, your organisation will simply undergo the process of mutation discussed earlier. Putting icing on top of a mud pie – the organisation and its products – won't make employees or customers enjoy the taste of what they are fed!

Richard Pascale is the author of *The Art of Japanese Management* (Penguin, 1981). He co-developed the 'Seven S Framework' (with Tom Peters), and in the 1970s he worked as a consultant to many Fortune 500 companies. His writings advocate instilling mental disciplines that will make people behave differently and then help them to sustain their new behaviour.

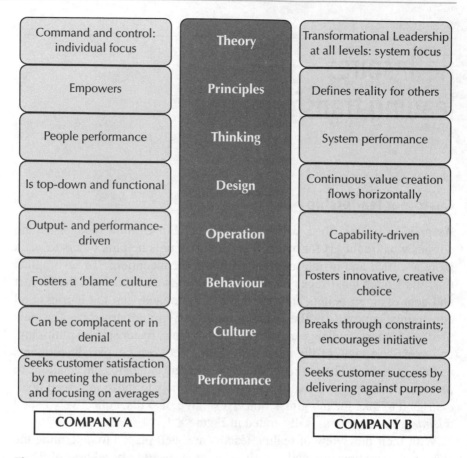

Company A		Company B
Command and control: individual focus	**Theory**	Transformational Leadership at all levels: system focus
Empowers	**Principles**	Defines reality for others
People performance	**Thinking**	System performance
Is top-down and functional	**Design**	Continuous value creation flows horizontally
Output- and performance-driven	**Operation**	Capability-driven
Fosters a 'blame' culture	**Behaviour**	Fosters innovative, creative choice
Can be complacent or in denial	**Culture**	Breaks through constraints; encourages initiative
Seeks customer satisfaction by meeting the numbers and focusing on averages	**Performance**	Seeks customer success by delivering against purpose

COMPANY A **COMPANY B**

Figure 8.1 Leadership spectrum

From a point of newly defined reality, pretence having been removed and the past having been put in the past, the organisation can move forward, seizing the opportunities and possibilities that are now in front of it. When the new Customer Leadership Culture begins to affect the organisational system and structures, working end to end to ensure that customer purpose is satisfied, change is set in motion. The business process and supporting functions start to transform; so do the reward and recognition systems; so do the product and services development. New technology is redesigned. And so on. When change throughout the organisation has reached a critical mass, and when the newly flexible foundations are in place that can lock onto customer demand, the pace of transformation becomes very rapid and at some point irreversible. At this point the origin of transformation has come to reside within the people – the staff and managers. It is no longer simply a pipe dream or an attractive theory; what was previously a pretence that things were fine has now become a reality.

Leadership at all levels

> Ordinary people doing extraordinary things
>
> Kasich (1999)

In most large organisations you can spot the leaders: they are usually gifted, charismatic people who can share their vision and command a following. They are extraordinary. Yet the leadership *we* hope for does not depend on extraordinary people – it depends on ordinary people who do extraordinary things.

In a Customer Value Enterprise®, leadership is at all levels. It is not about the person at the top, but about unlocking leadership throughout the organisation – from the person serving the customer at the frontline right up to senior management. Unlocking the leadership qualities of ordinary people across all levels of the organisation starts to release the organisation's true potential. Each leader will have a different message, each a different perspective, but all of them will share a common purpose. Transformational leaders in the organisation will articulate information and ideas across the spectrum of management, creating new possibilities for their colleagues, their customers and the organisation.

When most organisations attempt transformation, some merely rearrange their assets and resources and endeavour to reach new levels of performance and innovation. Despite this effort, however, the fundamental thinking – the building blocks of organisational design – remain unchanged. As described by Gary Fisher, Innovation Fellow at The Business Partnership Unit, Aston University, 'For those organisations it's like painting by numbers; the structure stays the same, they just change the colours.' Transformational leaders understand the existing structures but are not limited by them; as true artists, full of innovation and creativity, they aspire to paint their new picture of the world on a newly blank canvas. For them, anything is possible!

Leading by inspiration

In an organisation undergoing change, power resides with those individuals who can conceive a new view of the future and who can convey this view to others. In conversation with colleagues, they will express the possibilities that they themselves see in ways that can be understood and interpreted by their listeners, each from his or her own perspective. By successfully communicating these possibilities, they inspire others to take purposeful action in helping to develop an attractive and fulfilling working environment that their colleagues had not imagined to be possible. This image of leadership has been encapsulated perfectly by C. Wright Mills (1956), who explained:

> In our time, what is at issue is the very nature of humankind, the image we have of our limits and possibilities. History is not yet done with its exploration of the limits of what it means to be human.

When we talk about 'possibility' we mean a new view of reality that actively impacts people in the present time: a view that inspires, moves and touches people, and that invariably alters their view of working life itself, affecting their feelings and shaping their actions. Such possibilities, in which people have complete freedom of choice, are rarely experienced by people in society today. Shared leadership is not about exploitation or coercing people into doing things – that type of leadership is manipulation, and people recognise it straightaway.

Instead, shared leadership offers freedom, inspiration and transformation. Colleagues see in individual Transformational Leaders change that they find attractive, and feel inspired to take action for themselves. They see their colleagues' position of integrity, welcome it, and want to share in it.

This approach does not dictate the outcome – because there is no control or manipulation, the inspiration of Transformational Leaders will have whatever outcome the freedom of choice evokes from others. Staff see that they themselves can make a difference and are no longer prepared to sit back and wait for change: they join in actively creating it and incidentally inspire others as they share the view of reality and their new sense of possibility. Bit by bit, people at all levels come to terms with change and find their own ways of relating personally to the organisation's ongoing transformation.

People are inspired by many things in life. As Lao Tzu put it:

> The wicked leader is he whom the people despise. The good leader is he whom the people revere. The great leader is he of whom the people say, 'We did it ourselves.'
>
> 6th century BCE

Many people have been inspired by the work of Mother Teresa of Calcutta. While few felt drawn to embrace her specific cause, her example inspired them to embrace new activities of their own choosing. The work of

Mother Teresa, combined with her ability to show people a new way of seeing the world, motivated them to live out their own dreams and insights.

Leading for transformation

Leadership conversations are not like ordinary conversations. Transformational leaders have learned a valuable skill: they know how to break down resistance, how to free others from past experiences, and how to recognise the fixed beliefs underlying the language and behaviour of those with whom they speak. A leadership conversation maintains integrity, acknowledges reality, names pretences, draws attention to the costs to the organisation, the employee and the customer, and explores the idea that something different is possible.

Leaders stand in a position of honesty and present their view of reality to others with openness: 'This is what we pretend it's like, and this is the cost. And this is the possibility that we really want to make real. In order that this organisation can *create* this possibility, this is how we as leaders are going to be: tenacious, courageous, and honest.' The fact that leaders are asking nothing of other people but only of themselves is inspirational: staff will follow because they are inspired by somebody at last doing something about the pretence for which they will no longer have to pay the emotional cost. It is also inspirational for staff to learn that they no longer have to go against the grain of their own experience – that their experience and insights are now going to be valued by their managers; and that they themselves can make a difference, not just in what they *do* differently from now on, but also because of what they already *know*.

Not everybody can lead. Indeed, it takes courage, tenacity and honesty to put oneself in a position where one may be criticised, where colleagues might say, 'You've become a management crony.' It takes bravery to step into that position and present information that colleagues and managers may not want to hear. The conventional hierarchy seems often to be a constraint to newly developed leaders, who have to deal with the fact that there are different people on different levels and with different perspectives. What a true leader is able to do is to understand those different perspectives, and to converse with people at each level in a way that touches, moves and inspires them.

The form of leadership we are advocating is from an inspirational and a transformational standpoint, not from an authoritarian or conventional standpoint. Inevitably, *leadership and change just means having conversations – leadership conversations – hundreds of them; thousands of them; day in, day out*. And all of these conversations have a common perspective and a common purpose: one that brings integrity back into the organisation and that asks whether it is really delivering what matters in the eyes of its customers, its employees and its stakeholders.

Leadership conversations culminate in statements that propose a new reality in contrast with the view taken in the past. One such statement is this:

> To create opportunities for success through the provision of expert, unique and customer-driven solutions in a supportive and happy environment that enables freedom for all to prosper.

This was a place that they were truly inspired to create and one that inspired others to embark on a journey of change.

Gradually people begin to understand that it is their own responsibility to change their environment. The solution isn't just 'somebody else's problem'; it isn't just something that might happen sometime, maybe never; it isn't something that can be left to the management. It's a new way of working, and it will happen when *they* make it happen – when they themselves accept the responsibility.

Leading by example

Accepting leadership of oneself – changing one's very way of being – can be exhilarating. Staff learn to be completely authentic in every way, and in a way that touches and moves others and inspires them to take action.

Leaders take responsibility for themselves, and they take collective responsibility for the organisation. Whatever their position in the organisation, they capture customer intelligence and create change. They take ownership and accept responsibility for their actions, supported by customer data.

Finding common purpose

Most management textbooks and nearly all organisational-change books say that the first area in which to start organisational change is to *define a 'common organisational purpose'*. This 'common purpose' is often erroneously translated into simple aspirational terms such as 'To become number one in our industry' or 'To become the best in the class'.

To be truly effective, however, the common organisational purpose needs to integrate the aspirations of the many groups involved: the employees, the shareholders, the executive staff, and – most importantly – the customers, whose aspirations, or 'customer purpose', have first been researched and defined. With a customer-centric approach, by the very nature of 'sensing and responding', the common purpose can be defined only *after* you have gathered customer intelligence data – not before, as is so often the case.

Sustaining change

Encountering difficulties

Some organisations begin the transformational journey but fail to sustain their embrace of change. There are two main reasons for this, each of which may be compounded by self-doubt.

The first reason is loss of confidence in the process. Although they have defined reality and begun to reshape their environment based on customer demand, organisations may find that some of their activities fail to generate positive outcomes in the eyes of staff, managers or customers. The changes, if they happen at all, aren't rapid enough or don't reduce costs fast enough. Here are some typical comments:

- 'It's just another fad – we do this already.'
- 'You can't change how we measure the service.'
- 'Who's going to pay for this?'
- 'Our customers won't change the contract.'
- 'Customers will take advantage of us.'
- 'Staff will be out of control.'
- 'Jobs will be threatened.'
- 'Everyone else has to change first.'
- 'We tried this before – it hasn't worked.'
- 'All my customers are happy.'

Of course, these pressures may be coming from people who have not yet understood the new ways of measuring service or who consider that they have most to 'lose' from the transformation. They prefer a traditional focus on performance, and they start to apply pressure. These people aren't bad – they simply haven't embraced the new way of working. As well as these, though, there are always people within organisations who just wait for initiatives to fail, especially if this makes them look better – it's always easier to blame others for failing than to take responsibility for positive change oneself. In this situation, pretence creeps back and reality becomes blurred. The new leaders, although they still see the new possibilities in front of them, begin to doubt their ability to effect the change. In the face of continuing resistance they may revert to earlier characteristics and thinking patterns, and become stuck and disillusioned. Perhaps, they hope, someone else will be brave enough to make a difference.

The second reason why the transformational journey may not be sustained is loss of momentum. Although the organisation began by breaking through traditional structures and behavioural patterns, yielding impressive results and addressing organisational barriers, every obstacle removed has been replaced by further new possibilities or by even larger barriers – barriers of a kind never experienced before.

Despite their new-found abilities, leaders may begin to doubt their capacity to overcome the obstacles, and the voices of the past return to question their capability: 'What if, after all, all these problems are my responsibility?' At the forefront of change, working towards new possibilities and living with uncertainty, the leading edge of transformation can be a very lonely place.

A framework for mentoring and coaching

The journey for Transformational Leaders can be highly rewarding and at the same time frustrating. Convinced by the theory and having started out with conviction and excitement, they have set the transformation in motion throughout the organisation, and colleagues at all levels are now having conversations about a new way of working, uncovering poor practices, and learning to share leadership. But doubt creeps in when no visible dividend has yet emerged – as yet, no great savings, no immediate reduction in delivery time, no sudden surge in sales, and no clear abatement in restoration costs. Leaders can feel somewhat exposed, with little measurement of success or comparison.

Some leaders may begin to procrastinate, gradually reverting to old practices and retreating to their comfort zones. They may also be convinced by others that this, after all, is not the way forward – that it's too difficult, that nothing will change. This is what we call the 'rollercoaster of enthusiasm', and it occurs for leaders throughout the course of their transformational journey. When the whole world seems against them and change does not appear to be happening, leaders may find that their motivation in continuing to lead goes up and down repeatedly, and they may lose their self-belief.

It is not enough to create a new breed of leader and to set them off, hoping that they will simply forget all their old mental and behavioural habits and find the capability consistently to break through resistance. An organisation needs to set up a framework to support its leaders: a source of continual guidance for those who face insurmountable barriers. The framework should provide them with the *mentoring* and *coaching* they need to assure them of their direction and to give them a place where they can talk about how lonely and anxious they may feel. They also need an environment in which they feel free to be experimental both in their thinking and in their practice, and to share their innovations with co-leaders without fear of failure or ridicule.

Enthusiasm and benefit

What leaders experience and begin to understand is that within every transformation there is a natural rhythm (Figure 8.2). First there is a period of enthusiasm and momentum: a spark of excitement and drive to create a new way of working, even though the benefits of the work may not be immediately apparent.

However, it takes time to lay the foundations and to begin to change organisational structures and thinking, to share customer intelligence data with individuals, and to help everyone cut across functions to create the possibility that others can take action; and this time lag will be interpreted by some leaders as 'Things just aren't working.' These leaders may start to fear that they are doing the wrong things and may go through a phase of resignation, blame or denial.

Successful leaders, though, will continue despite their discomfort, backing their belief, at heart, that the benefits will eventually begin to show. And indeed they may have to wait: but although the benefits don't come until some time later, when they *do* come there is no going back, and all the enthusiasm is regained ... until the next crisis comes along, and the sequence happens all over again.

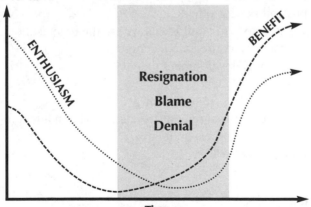

Figure 8.2 Enthusiasm and benefit cycle

To ensure the success of the transformation and what underpins the creation of the Customer Value Enterprise®, therefore, it is vital that the coaching and mentoring framework is in place to support leaders through these ups and downs.

The Transformational Leader

Characteristics

The Transformational Leaders created by the Journey to Customer Purpose have a remarkable set of characteristics, listed below. As you read the list, think about your own situation: if instilled in your staff, what difference would these characteristics make to *your* organisation?

A Transformational Leader:

■ thinks differently
■ views the organisation as if a customer
■ understands and describes reality for others
■ provides customer intelligence data
■ predicts customer satisfaction
■ identifies what matters to the clients' organisations
■ identifies new opportunities in customer demand
■ fosters innovation
■ creates leadership conversations
■ deals with organisational constraints and conflicts
■ understands resistance to change
■ challenges conventional perspectives and decision-making patterns
■ creates possibilities for others
■ has the capacity to lead at all levels within the organisation
■ identifies obstacles to effective leadership
■ creates operational development plans
■ redesigns processes
■ redesigns the working environment
■ creates end-to-end measurements related to what matters to customers
■ applies new customer measurements
■ eliminates corporate waste.

Providing leadership

Creating leadership is an aspect of transformational change traditionally thought of as something done by the Human Resources department, or as something that will just will 'happen' when the organisation has fixed its structure and its performance issues. The biggest cost to organisations today arises from neglecting to focus on the behaviour, knowledge and experience of employees, on their ability to work through barriers and constraints, and on their ability to articulate the customer reality and to initiate leadership conversations. Employees hold so much wisdom, yet the organisation neglects to learn from it.

There is a profound difference between organisations that harness human intelligence and organisations that do not. The human intelligence of existing staff in their present roles – along with the removal of institutionalised constraints – is what is needed to drive change through the entire organisation, to create the conditions for flexibility in a customer-driven world, and to begin the journey to create a Customer Value Enterprise®.

PART V

The Journey to Customer Purpose: Re-Create

Introduction

Gary Fisher, MA, CIPD
Innovation Fellow, The Business Partnership Unit,
Aston University

The key differentiator in the 21st-century marketplace for organisations in the developed world is innovative value creation. Indeed, cost-reduction strategies supported by mass-production methodologies will only pay dividends to those organisations that either automate or relocate to low labour cost economies. The question is, therefore, how do organisations aspiring to employ people across the developed world evolve and move up the value chain?

Are Customer Value Principles viable? The authors demonstrate not only viability but a pathway to creating highly responsive organisations. The cost-efficiency mindset merely processes customers through a limited number of predetermined channels designed either to pacify or to remedy the disappointed at the lowest cost.

Through sensing and responding to customer needs, it is recognised that the vast majority of service work is the result of organisational shortcomings. Customer intelligence is used both to eliminate waste and to inform future organisational strategy. Customer demand-based innovation must become common practice.

The practical application of this approach establishes highly skilled, highly autonomous employees capable of capturing customer intelligence and seeking new ways to create value. This has not only changed behaviours and activities but also engendered a transformation in management style. Control and compliance is systematically replaced in favour of support and facilitation.

Whilst customer-centric, customer relationship management and 'employees are our most valued asset' rhetoric is common, it is rare to find a workplace reality where customer value and human intelligence instigate the reduction of costs and increase revenue. The macro-economic imperative to adapt or decline is knocking on the door of the business world. Soon the door will be forced wide open. The question is, do we have the sense to respond?

CHAPTER 9

Re-Create:
an organisation that self-develops

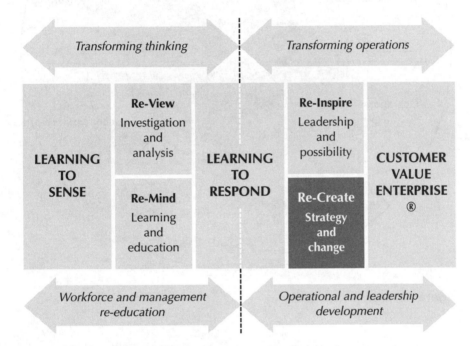

Figure 9.1 The Journey to Customer Purpose: Re-Create

Focusing on customers

To be effective in creating a true Customer Value Enterprise®, all activities need to be aligned to customer purpose by ensuring that all the key decisions within the business are related to creating customer success. Instead of designing *development*, design *organisational self-development*.

The realignment of the corporate plumbing is essential to true customer-centricity and creates business and personal benefits. Unless all areas that interact with the customer are diagnosed there will be disconnects across

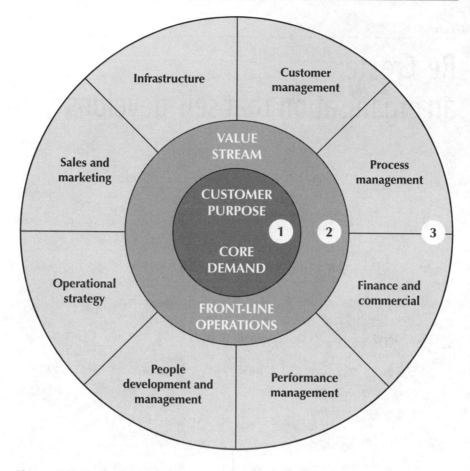

Figure 9.2 Customer-centricity

functions and within departments, and the customer will experience the consequences of these disconnects (Cutcher-Gershenfeld and Ford, 2005). Understanding how to align all activities to the needs of customers is what makes customer-centricity possible. All components of the enterprise are aligned to create customer value (Figure 9.2).

People-development programmes also need alignment with customer purpose: these give the workforce the attributes they need to initiate change. *Sales and marketing* functions need to adjust to meet the flexible needs of the customer. Measurements need to align with performance, as judged from the customer perspective, and new *performance management metrics* emerge. In the supporting areas, the *infrastructure* needs alignment with new processes and activities; and then informed decisions can be made, based on customer intelligence data, with regard to the introduction of new tools, the configuration of existing ones, and the potential business outcomes of their adjustment. At the same time, the organisation must adopt a different *operational strategy* to remain continually responsive – a strategy that engenders the *capture of customer value* and the *removal of waste*. Financial and commercial activities have to move towards customer-centricity so that they can remain locked onto customer needs; this also creates the incentive to improve service provision and take out negative demand. This is monitored through developing new accountancy practices which capture the inter-operability of all activities and measure business outcomes end-to-end and not just those of local budget holders.

We do not advocate standardisation by *process*, however, but standardisation by *method* and *approach*. Each organisation has its own internal functions, each of which may have its own customer proposition. What we are outlining, therefore, is a method rather than a recipe. The customer brings different ingredients each time, and seeks a unique outcome that fits specific requirements: using this method the organisation can meet the customer's requirements. If you standardise on the ingredients, the same recipe will provide all your customers with the same cake; but if instead you ask the customer to specify the ingredients and use a proven method, you will bake a cake they actually want.

By adopting this approach you can also sense and respond to the needs of the organisation itself, creating systematic change and organisational development and flexibility.

Developing the people

Identifying training needs

At the heart of any truly responsive organisation are the people who serve customers. Their development and ongoing training are critical to the sustainability of an on-demand service, in which the essence of the work is to use the innate talent of staff to converse with the customer about his or her world, to capture customer intelligence, and then to act on this data.

The CORE Demand profile can be used to identify training needs. When the organisation fully understands its customer demand profile, it may find that current training is in fact institutionalising waste. Returning to our tyre-fixing analogy, it may be that the organisation is providing its people with training in the use of tyre-fixing equipment when it is the road that is the cause of the problems. For example, it might be that rather than training all frontline staff to fix tyres, resources would be better spent in additional training for two employees in the organisation who are careless about dropping glass on the forecourt. It is clearly a poor use of resources to train people to carry out wasteful activity more effectively. Training staff to respond to restorative demand just increases costs and locks in user dissatisfaction.

Nevertheless, some restorative demand will inevitably arise and so someone must be trained to deal with it in the short term while the organisation is removing the demand in the medium and long term. The principle is two-fold: first, to restore value as quickly as possible; and second, moving on from that, to remove the cause instead of institutionalising the repair.

Defining the training requirements on the basis of the CORE Demand profile will ensure that money is spent on developing staff to service customers effectively and to serve the organisation efficiently. The trainers can also demonstrate a clear link between the training activity and any *change* in the demand profile. It can be focused on developing employees' awareness of customer value and organisational waste, and engendering in them a sense of responsibility and confidence that they can improve value creation and remove the waste. In this way training can be directly linked to real business needs.

Moving work, not people

Below, in the section called 'Shifting capability to creating value', we write about 'Moving value creation closer to the customer', a concept that is critical to the training and development plan. Due to functional specialisation, staff are usually trained to move into other departments that have different specialities. Often such moves are accompanied by horse-trading between managers who don't want to lose good staff from their domain and staff who quite understandably wish to increase their skills and their rewards. While in many cases this is unavoidable, there may be an alternative: instead of training people to move between departments, you can train staff to move the work. This is a very different skill and its adoption has many advantages.

It is usually the case that more highly paid members of staff work further away from the customer interface than lower-paid staff. In moving the work from higher-paid staff to lower-paid staff, therefore, not only do you reduce the cost of delivery, but you may also reduce the end-to-end delivery time, in some cases by as much as 70 per cent. By training staff to move work closer to the customer you are incidentally freeing up the time of higher-paid staff downstream to whom you can give other higher-level work. This approach frees up senior-level staff, who can take on additional responsibilities. This is a win–win–win situation: the customer, the employee and the business all benefit. Training and development, which are key to encouraging this kind of cross-functional co-operation, can promote teamwork and help to sever management ties to 'functional specialisation'.

This approach therefore encourages multi-skilling and resource optimisation, without the need to move people around the organisation. CORE Demand data and customer intelligence provide points of reference, a 'north star' by which to steer customer-centric training plans. When the organisation's demand profile changes, it has by definition to change its response profile also. For demand management to be effective, the collective thinking of operations and the training department must keep changing in line with new customer demands.

Nurturing innate talent

Over time, training becomes more and more customer-centric. However, the job design and the reward and recognition systems also need to change in alignment.

Encouragement for staff to remove waste and to increase value needs to be supported by the organisation's reward and recognition systems. If existing performance measurements are based on resourcing and cost metrics, then people will continue to pay attention to the old way of working. A new norm is needed: one that rewards and recognises staff for reducing waste, for reducing end-to-end cycle time, for innovation and for value creation.

Job roles need to be designed with enough flexibility to allow continuous upskilling. Staff can be given incentives to remove work and to perform higher-level tasks without the need to move between departments. (See Figure 9.9, 'Moving value creation closer to the customer'.)

The creation of an open culture in which operational difficulties are discussed freely is essential to sustaining improvement and attacking resistance to change. As discussed in the 'Re-Inspire' chapters, the type of leadership needed in a Customer Value Enterprise® means that people-development plans must include coaching and mentoring in how to hold conversations about 'the art of possibility' (Zander and Zander, 2000). People at all levels will get stuck from time to time, fearful that highlighting organisational deficiencies might become career-limiting. Having access to a confidential, trusted network of coaches or mentors gives confidence and encourages the exploration of sensitive approaches to change.

Retaining a skilled workforce

If you succeed in creating an adaptive, confident workforce capable of innovation, you are inevitably increasing their marketability also. Staff who are most useful to your organisation will also be considered useful by your competitors. Your organisation faces this dilemma: does it want good staff who need to be rewarded properly if they are to be retained, or staff whom no one wants and who have to be constantly remotivated?

In maintaining a highly effective customer-focused workforce, the nurture and management of their talent becomes essential. As they gain skills and experience, staff will become ever more marketable. Nevertheless, they will usually stay loyal to the organisation because they will have come to relish working in an environment that encourages their full participation, and most would find it difficult to replicate this in other organisations.

Developing sales and marketing

In truly customer-centric organisations, the functions of sales and marketing are turned on their heads. Sales staff learn to have new conversations with customers about customer purpose, which drive informed decisions and the uptake of service. Marketing learns to drive new propositions to market by connecting with the customer intelligence captured by frontline operations and providing an innovative service offering.

Customer intelligence data and marketing intelligence

Traditionally marketing is disconnected from customer-facing operations; instead, it is outwardly aligned to the industry or to market segments within which the organisation's services operate. Marketing uses current industry profiles to predict potential revenue streams and to shape new offerings to market. These profiles are the source of the market intelligence that influences organisational decisions around new emerging strategies and product development. This same market intelligence is then devolved to product and service design teams who create new customer offerings; these in turn translate into new offerings and new operating procedures for frontline teams.

Customer intelligence data creates a customer view of service provision. It defines service effectiveness and predicts uptake based on current profiles of demand, which include data related to existing opportunity demand for new service and innovation. Proposition development is based on industry trends which can be tested against the current customer demand profile and customer demands captured by frontline operations. When designing new propositions against existing 'opportunity' demand, it becomes possible to predict the likelihood of their success, thereby reducing the risk to the business of new service introduction.

Although in reality they already have *known* customer demands, most organisations make no connection between gathering customer demand at the frontline and translating that into new propositions to market – the customer intelligence data stays in the realm of operational staff only. Clearly this is wasteful: the role of marketing should be solidly aligned with frontline operations, the ears and eyes of the organisation and thus the source of essential and reliable intelligence data. In a Customer Value Enterprise® marketing functions draw on a new organisational structure that 'pulls' customer intelligence data and responds by creating new service offerings already known to be desired, instead of creating demand by 'pushing' services to meet predicted consumption based on market trends.

Even so, however, it is not easy to push against the plethora of analysts' reports predicting market trends. The organisation's marketing department will need to be strongly convinced of the customer data if it is to support the organisation's propositions in what may be a sceptical or adverse environment in which objections may be raised by market analysts. The innovations, though, are based on solid customer data; and if it persists, the organisation will create an edge for this service.

Customer intelligence data and sales

Many traditional sales organisations sell from a menu of possible propositions, making presentations, offering opinions, and relying heavily on creating or maintaining personal relationships. The sales cycle is characterised by the need to convince and to handle objections. In organisations that collect customer intelligence, in contrast, you will find the sales people actively talking to frontline staff in order to gain insight into what is happening on the ground – what are the issues and what are the opportunities that could be developed (Bosworth and Holland, 2004).

Using data that underpins the CORE Demand profile, a salesperson can talk to prospects from a current knowledgeable perspective – not just trading opinions as before, but using up-to-date data. Because the CORE data is constructed around insight into the real needs of customers, the salesperson can discuss solutions to real problems in a contextual way, asking relevant questions rather than making offerings, and seeking to satisfy clients' overall business outcomes rather than merely selling in response to an obvious and immediate expressed need.

Conversations of this kind require questioning techniques and leadership abilities quite different from those needed for the traditional sales operation, in which the salesperson concentrates on trying to match offerings from the organisation's existing menu to customers' problems or apparent needs.

The difference in conversational style reflects a distinct difference in purpose: whereas the *traditional* sales team may simply sell services that their organisation knows it can manage and keep profitable, irrespective of the nature of the demand they are processing, the *customer-centric* sales team learns to listen carefully to customer requirements and then to translate these into a new menu of services, using this new data to inform the design of service provision and to dictate how operational teams manage customer transactions. Customer demand is thus profiled from the outset.

This approach to selling ensures the alignment of the entire organisation's resources to meet customer needs: no one will discover at the 'go-live' date that the profile of incoming demand and the requirements of service provision were inaccurate. Traditionally, the translation of a sales lead to design of service is related to driving output, efficiency and profitability; in the new approach service is designed against creating value, removing waste, and utilising customer intelligence data to predict customer sales decisions.

An organisation that focuses on understanding the sale from the customer's point of view, based on customer success and current customer demand, may sometimes take an informed decision not to tender for a specific piece of work. This is particularly likely if it is discovered that the potential work needs to be designed in a way that supports the processing of negative demand, as the organisation already understands that there is no customer value, little opportunity for incremental business opportunity, and the prospect of a defensive customer relationship.

The sales teams focused on relating to customer purpose will make opportunities to educate the customer to expect a new level of service, a new way of managing and measuring service provision, and a new method of delivering what the customer wants. Customers are not always conversant with this concept; however, it stimulates curiosity which in turn engenders conversations about service provision and new sales opportunities. With customer knowledge and intelligence data, organisations have the confidence to predict and outline customer desires and requirements, and to start the move away from traditional SLAs and KPIs, the usual contracted agreements and level of service and performance that are simply based on output and efficiency, rather than on business outcomes and customer success.

Performance management

Performance management – help or hindrance?

It is desirable that an organisation remains focused on delivering customer success and that it embraces the entire innovation of all the individuals.

Yet there is a dangerous challenge to the organisation that can lie unnoticed: poor performance management. Many organisations' performance techniques, instead of delivering positive customer outcomes that meet a common purpose, actually produce damaging and counterproductive behaviours. They become a means of controlling employees and monitoring their ability to process work, and organisations lose sight of the relationship between efficiency and effectiveness.

Organisational performance needs to be evaluated using measurements related to customer purpose and business outcome, rather than traditional measurements related to the means of output or solely to productivity. Purpose-related measurements will challenge the organisation's capability to respond to customer needs and will reveal the dysfunctionality of current measurement systems.

The people and the system

People are the integral ingredient in ensuring the entire success of these principles: there is simply no point in introducing these principles unless the organisation is capable of treating its people differently. For an organisation to consider changing its approach to understanding, measuring and rewarding individuals' performance can be a daunting and uncomfortable prospect, but it needs to happen.

As we have said already, most people-performance targets are introduced to demonstrate whether people are being productive enough, meeting contractual agreements, delivering a good customer experience, and so forth. That's the intention; and performance targets are used because organisations have been conditioned to see these outcomes as the ones that matter, and targets as the only way to evaluate the outcomes. As we now know, however, each individual's ability to perform is in fact inextricably linked to the environment or 'system' that surrounds them.

Evidence suggests that 80–90 per cent of organisational performance is a direct result of the organisational structures themselves, not the staff. Focusing on staff to increase operational performance can achieve no more than 10–20 per cent (Figure 9.3).

Purpose-related measurements, as previously discussed, focus people at all levels on delivering the business outcomes that lead to customer success. At first sight this may seem an extremely complicated method, but in practice it is simple to create a top-level view of end-to-end capability using the principles of CORE Demand management and profiling. We are not advocating that all efficiency measurements are wrong, however: we advocate that they should not be used to incentivise staff such as frontline operations.

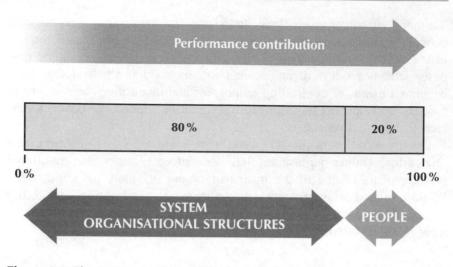

Figure 9.3 The 80:20 rule of organisational performance

These staff cannot improve their performance without making changes in aspects of the system over which they may have little control.

The new frontline function needs to be goaled against *creating value*; managers should be goaled against *creating capability to deliver value* – not simply output, but the means to produce output.

Enterprise performance

The Customer Value Enterprise® needs to takes a holistic view of its combined organisational resource and its ability to continually lock onto customer needs and deliver against customer purpose; together, these are the measure of its *enterprise performance*. This approach creates a new way of looking at how the work operates across all departmental boundaries, and highlights impacts and development opportunities. This will lead to the systematic realignment of the infrastructure to meet customer purpose, using customer intelligence data and end-to-end measurement as the yardsticks for change – see Figure 9.4.

When the flow, demand profile and end-to-end cycle time for responding to demand are all determined – from the customer right through operations and the rest of the supporting service providers – new ways of managing, measuring and reporting become apparent. The demand profile not only identifies responsiveness but provides the customer context by which operational effectiveness will be judged by the customer, so informed strategies,

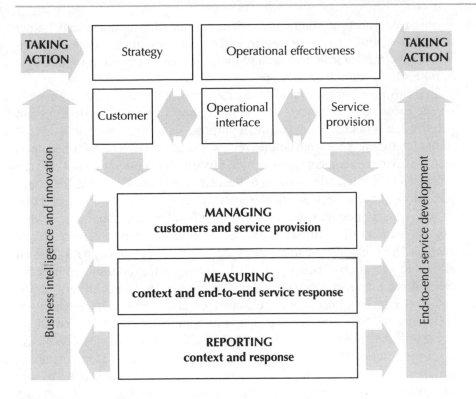

Figure 9.4 Strategy to performance: managing, measuring, reporting, taking action

direction and improvements can be made. Piece by piece, the organisation will systematically align itself to the needs of the customer. A very clear view will emerge of what the corporate plumbing looks like: intelligence from the customer perspective will make obvious where action needs to be taken.

Customer management

The management of customer relationships cannot be taken for granted: service must be continually linked to customers' strategic objectives. Merely espousing the mantra of customer-centricity or 'putting the customer at the heart of the organisation' is not enough: the organisation must keep addressing the real *purpose* of customer interaction, seeking continually to understand why customers use its products and services and to what use they put them.

In a traditional mass-production organisation a customer manager is constrained by conventional organisational structures and measurements.

Focused on meeting contractual efficiency targets, numbers and output efficiencies, with staff powerless to make improvements because they cannot change the environment around them, it can be tempting to make the numbers look better than they are.

In a customer-centric organisation, the focus of customer management is on the nature of the transaction and the removal of negative demand and activity that is not related to customer purpose. Conversations centre on customer intelligence data that defines reality and is the basis of informed decisions. Service agreements are directed towards business outcomes and are grounded by a true understanding of the origins of cost. Consider, for example, an IT service provider to the aircraft industry: it is no longer good enough to talk about how many printers are fixed in a set timeframe – what matters is rather the business impact if passengers cannot board an aircraft because their boarding cards cannot be printed, including the knock-on effects of the aircraft being grounded, consequential boarding delays for other aircraft, and damaged customer expectation. In the health service, for instance, conversations should no longer be about why patients can't get appointments with doctors and how the appointments system could be improved: they need to be focused on why patients need to transact with the doctor and whether this is truly necessary. For example, does a disabled patient really need to see the doctor to begin an authorisation process to verify a disability in order to obtain a disabled parking permit?

In principle, organisations understand that without customers they would be out of business. In practice, though, the way they have traditionally been designed, built and operated leads to misinterpretation of true customer needs and to a shortfall in the provision of service. Instead of creating services that continually meet the *entire* needs of customers, they create services that 'push' customers to transact as the organisation wishes them to. Conversations with customers become centred on responding to negative demand. This leaves organisations with a need to recover the situation and to find attractive ways to retain customers who have lost value.

From the conventional customer management perspective, processing negative demand provides an increased opportunity to enhance the customer experience, and organisations thrive on this cycle of negative experience. They overlook the likelihood that other service providers may generate products and services that continually create positive outcomes and customer success – products and services that may remove existing revenue from their own market. Conversations about customers become cynical and resigned: 'We can never meet all their needs – they demand too much.' Too often, the self-justification for lost custom relates to price, not service. Organisations can find infinite ways of being price-competitive and ignoring the true nature of service demand; eventually they become just a commodity, and in the marketplace today commodities can easily be replaced or switched. Today organisations can no longer compete solely on price, and it's no longer even about creating positive experiences – what matters today is managing customer service in a way that creates customer success and positive business outcomes.

Restoring demand in the context of negative customer experience has become a major industry and is considered normal practice. End-to-end organisational structures become locked into this way of managing customer relationships.

A new relationship with customers

What is needed is a new relationship with customers: a new way of managing client success, with conversations based on CORE Demand data. In a customer-centric organisation, staff will focus on activity that highlights constraints within both their customers' and their organisation's environments.

Paradoxically, when organisations focus on removing the origins of cost, they release locked-in costs of producing, managing and servicing entirely preventable transactions. As well as increasing the value customers receive, customer loyalty and new possibilities for service diversification and innovation are created.

Environment costs

Figures 9.5–9.8 illustrate the typical phases of service development and outline the customer management focus during the transition to reduce environment costs and increase revenue and customer responsiveness.

Phase 1 shows customer demand coming into a service environment that has several functional 'areas' (the black rectangles in Figure 9.5), which deal with different aspects of customer transactions. For example, a contact-centre environment could have a call reception and logging department which passes work on to a second group which validates information or maybe collects customer history and then sends this on to a third department for final resolution by a specialist. This tiered approach is often referred to as 'first line' (or 'frontline'), 'second line', 'third line', and so on. Most organisations find that work cannot be processed cleanly on first pass, and on many occasions a simple transaction can be passed back and forth between departments until resolution.

The skill and capability of people to *resolve* the transaction may reside in the fourth-line function, yet 'filters' are created by departments that prioritise

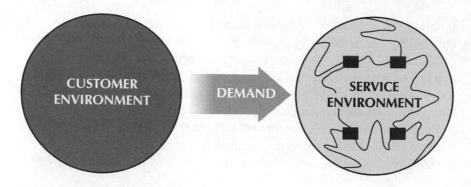

Figure 9.5 Environment costs: phase 1 (*adapted from Gharajedaghi, 1999*)

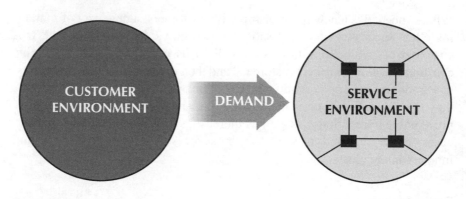

Figure 9.6 Environment costs: phase 2

incoming demand and 'sift' it into the correct 'blocks' for resolution. The wavy lines in Figure 9.5 represent the organisational 'waste' in terms of ineffective processes, inadequate training, slow IT systems, and the like.

Conversations when managing the customer relationship in this phase are focused on cost and capability of resolving incoming demand within current service agreements. Although demands are being met, the customer often proclaims that the service provider is not being innovative and is not feeding back intelligence to enhance the customer's environment and the customer's experience.

Phase 2 of organisational development (Figure 9.6) occurs when the service organisation comes under increased pressure to reduce costs, to provide competitive prices, and to guarantee the reduction of the cost of service provision to the customer. The organisation's initial focus is often to reduce the cost of its own environment by taking out the 'slack' and changing

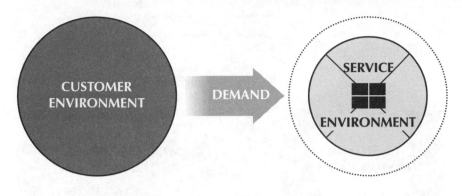

Figure 9.7 Environment costs: phase 3

or removing people's roles, consolidating processes, and often investing in technology to optimise the processing of incoming demand. Customer management conversations at this point are seen as innovative: they provide the customer with a solution by committing the organisation to a cheaper and more focused service provision. They yield customer relationship information related to the nature of demand received, but they fail to ask why the demand is generated in the first place. This period of perceived innovation is short-lived.

In Phase 3 (Figure 9.7), as service organisations feel even more pressure to innovate and to reduce the cost of operating, passing on a reduction in price to the customer, they begin to consolidate functions further. This phase may involve co-locating departments, cross-training staff, and providing innovative technology and process solutions to streamline activity.

Costs are now at an all-time low, but the organisation has immobilised itself: it has come to a point where it is susceptible to 'falling over' in reaction to fluctuating customer demand, and the service often starts to fail. The service organisation tries to recover a positive relationship with the customer, but it may be seen by the customer as too late: often the customer pulls out and finds an alternative service provider, or the service organisation has to increase its resources and costs to correct the failure. The service organisation becomes stuck and falls into a perpetual cycle of managing service failures and negative demand. This leads to a defensive relationship with the customer. There is a solution, but it is not apparent to a conventional organisation.

Phase 4 of organisational development (Figure 9.8) faces up to the fundamental reason why service environment costs are high – the incoming customer demand. As we have said earlier, if organisations moved away from designing to meet *all* incoming demand, they could reduce the processing of

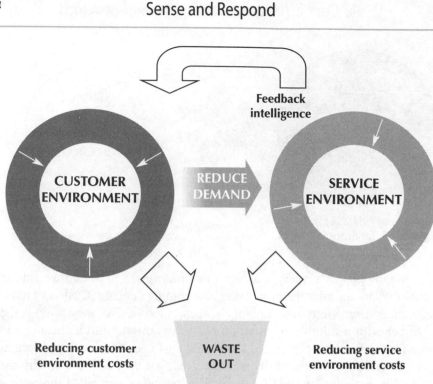

Figure 9.8 Environment costs: phase 4

demand by between 40 and 90 per cent. For service organisations this equates to millions of pounds, yet it goes unnoticed.

Suppose, then, that the organisation addresses this problem. It analyses the nature of incoming customer demand and removes entirely preventable transactions. Organisational costs will reduce; customer value creation will be optimised. The management of customer service is now based on conversations that relate to customer intelligence – how to remove the barriers that cause unwanted customer demand, and how to remove waste both for the customer and for the service environment. The service organisation, standing in this place of integrity, can have realistic conversations about how to remove barriers that cause unwanted demand in their own environment, and consequently it can agree to new service levels that take into account the reduced waste and increased value.

Shifting capability to creating value

One of the impressive aspects of organisations designed on mass-production principles is that they can achieve critical mass and then reduce operating costs.

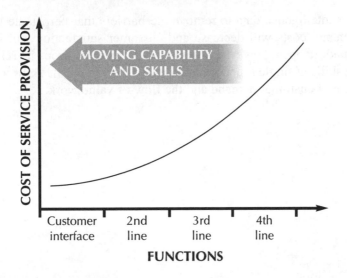

Figure 9.9 Moving value creation closer to the customer

However, getting critical mass around a function is a thing of the past: the new approach creates the achievement of critical mass around the *flow of work* – around what creates value for the customer.

This means that skills do not stay in specialised areas; instead, skills move to the appropriate place that creates value. Skills must be aligned to the logical non-stop flow of value creation at the right point in the process, rather than stopping and starting the work and batching it up for transport to a specialist area. There are times when specialisation is necessary or unavoidable, but its application must form part of the continuous flow processes.

Another problem is the degree to which specialisation has grown. For instance, some organisations will segment the organisation of work by customer groups, by brands, or even by levels of customer spend. However, this segmentation may have nothing to do with the nature of the actual work that arrives. In reality the segmented groups may be dealing with exactly the same customer demand. As a result, the management and duplication of work processes and technology are maintained to process demand in this specialised, segmented way. This does not create value for the customer, and it adds costs to the business and increases customer frustration. This very specialisation amplifies the amount of effort required to process existing work and itself generates additional unwanted and preventable demand from disgruntled customers.

When an organisation works systematically to remove preventable demand, shifts the capability to respond to creating value, and feeds back customer intelligence data to remove the barriers that perpetuate unnecessary demand, costs will decrease and customer satisfaction will increase. This cannot happen, however, unless the organisation drops its reliance on keeping skills in single functions and instead distributes the skills to support the nature of customer demand and the flow of value work.

CHAPTER 10

Re-Create:
customer-centric management

Infrastructure

Old certainties and structures are continually being swept away by the pace of technological progress, such as the provision of online internet services. These advances place enormous demands on an organisation's IT infrastructure and application support, which must be planned and built with continuous adaptability in mind; it must be flexible and scalable, so that it can meet the changing needs of the organisation and its customers.

New supply channels

The customer is now increasingly involved in the production process itself. For example, a major computer company allows customers to select and configure equipment options online, and to track delivery progress in the same way. This type of service is excellent for the knowledgeable customer, but can be quite intimidating to customers who lack the necessary computer knowledge or who do not have the time or inclination to choose and configure equipment themselves.

New technology is not enough

The traditional model usually seeks to use technologies to replace service staff. In this book we have demonstrated conclusively that this approach, if not centred around customer needs, will increase costs for all concerned, will lock in frustration for the user, and will encourage service providers to maintain their status as corporate waste-disposal units.

The technology itself is not usually at fault: it is simply that many companies are automating demand that should be removed, or even in some cases using the technology to transport work to low-cost labour economies in an effort to reduce costs. In the long term it does not matter which location actually serves customer demand: the issue is one of value creation and removing waste.

Insights from CORE Demand data

CORE Demand data not only measures end-to-end performance: it also incorporates crucial customer feedback that enables improvement at the point of service provision and can be used to drive services toward higher-value solutions at lower costs.

When a business has been evaluated using a combination of CORE Demand data and end-to-end response measurements, an assessment can be made as to the efficacy of IT in assisting in the creation of value and removing waste. Technology should be an enabler, reducing end-to-end processing time in addition to providing information on operational performance.

Changing customer demand and the increasing pace of technological complexity mean that one requires an anchor point from which to take bearings. The CORE data provides this, giving direction in a chaotic environment.

Many companies that implement new technologies fail to understand the nature of demand from their customers, and get frustrated when the technology does not bring the expected returns. As well as misunderstanding the nature of demand, companies sometimes fail to take into account the actual effort required to move the company onto new technologies and to change working practices.

Carrying out a CORE Demand analysis *prior to implementation* would provide both qualitative and quantitative data with which to make an investment case – data that could mitigate risks. More importantly, the CORE Demand analysis involves frontline staff in defining the technology requirements and their subsequent job roles. When the time comes to implement the technology, the staff are ready and willing to pull it from technology suppliers. (This is in contrast to the traditional approach: communicate, push, negotiate, resist.) The pre- and post-implementation status can be checked using the same CORE Demand profile and end-to-end measurements.

Having investigated and defined the CORE Demand profile, many companies use technology to assist service staff in the collection, collation and reporting of the demand. In addition to product and service codes, it is advisable to create user-defined codes for frontline staff – demand profiles will be in a constant state of change, with old ones disappearing and new ones emerging, so the coding system needs to be able to flex in concert with these changes.

Once the demand types have been defined, evaluations can be made as to which is the appropriate channel for delivery. At this point, organisations would not want to automate restorative demand unless every attempt has first been made to remove it at source. The other demand types – under the broad headings of creation, opportunity and external – can now be provided for.

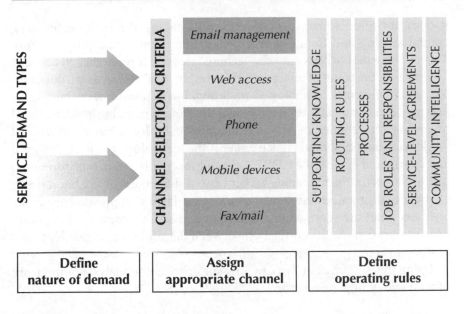

Figure 10.1 Multimedia channel strategy

The CORE Demand profile provides a basis upon which to construct a multimedia 'delivery channel strategy' (Figure 10.1). Take time to evaluate how each demand type would be processed:

1 define the nature of the demand type and any sub-demands;
2 define channel selection criteria;
3 define the operating rules.

Select the appropriate channel to service the particular demand type, taking into consideration such factors as security, urgency, complexity of content, and sophistication of user. Then define the supporting knowledge, work-routing rules, support processes, job roles and responsibilities. Service-level agreements should be set according to demand type and channel, not a blanket agreement (such as 'Respond to all e-mails within 24 hours').

Technology – transition – transformation

To gain an appreciation of the implementation effort needed, we have applied what we call the *3-T's* model: *technology – transition – transformation*. This model is intended to assist conversations about effort and resourcing;

it does not offer a precise science. Simply taking the basic technology, commissioning and testing it will take 20 per cent of the project effort. Transitioning the business onto new technologies will take another 30 per cent.

However, the result of all this effort is simply 'business as usual, done better'. More often new technologies are brought in to transform the business – and may even be a catalyst in creating a different type of business. For staff to exploit the features of new technologies calls for a transformation of workforce practices: this is much easier if the technology has been designed and configured against the CORE Demand profile. It is this *transformation* that accounts for the remaining 50 per cent of the project effort, but it is this element that produces the most valuable and lasting improvements to the business. Staff are more willing to accept and adapt to new working practices as they can see the correlation between their jobs, the technology, and customer needs.

Using the 3-T's model, we can now summarise our analysis of the work of technology implementation:

- **Technology** *20 per cent of the total effort*
  - taking a standard build out of the box
  - commissioning
  - testing

- **Transition** *30 per cent of the total effort*
  - making a business case
  - communication
  - demand analysis
  - channel strategy
  - business requirements
  - process definition and transfer
  - service-level agreements
  - training

- **Transformation** *50 per cent of the total effort*
  - new end-to-end measurements
  - exploitation of tools and systems
  - systematically collecting and acting on intelligence data

Customer-centric operational strategy

Operational strategy is influenced by wide-ranging activities, and may include strategic planning, change management, programme deployment and project management, together with organisational design and operating methods.

What we advocate is that true customer-centric organisations have the capability to lock onto customer purpose and that they learn to integrate all strategic activity so that it has one common characteristic – to align the entire organisation's resources to meet customer needs, including the gathering of customer intelligence at the frontline and the use of this intelligence in influencing strategic and systematic change. Customer-facing operations should recognise their responsibility for providing the intelligence to determine future strategies and development activity, and should use CORE Demand data to establish criteria for success.

CORE operational development

By understanding customer purpose and value an organisation can build a clear picture of the interactions between the various strategic activities, and can thereby ascertain the most successful combination of effort that will optimise successful implementation and create sustained development.

It is a strategic decision to place responsibility with frontline operations. This allows the organisation to utilise frontline analysis and investigation techniques to produce CORE Demand data that can determine the success of a given activity. The CORE Demand profile is capable of producing a business case for change: management can make informed decisions, and operations can predict activity outcomes, operational costs, potential revenues, and the organisation's capability to respond. This in turn creates a sense of assurance and focuses key resources on the creation and development of successful strategies that yield demonstrably positive results.

Operations step into the role of responsibility and influence the organisation's dynamics: this begins to transform the organisation's design. Change is driven by CORE customer demand data, which is the basis for any decisions around service improvement and operational development (Figure 10.2).

From a strategic point of view, frontline operations need to have the autonomy to identify and remove the origins of waste and any barriers that lock in restorative demand and cause unnecessary processing. Operations have responsibility for optimising processes and the flow of positive demand, and for presenting customer intelligence data to product and service development teams. These teams gain insight into the scope of opportunity and innovate new service offerings and sales propositions; in turn, customer management teams rethink current agreements with customers and suppliers to avoid processing external negative demand.

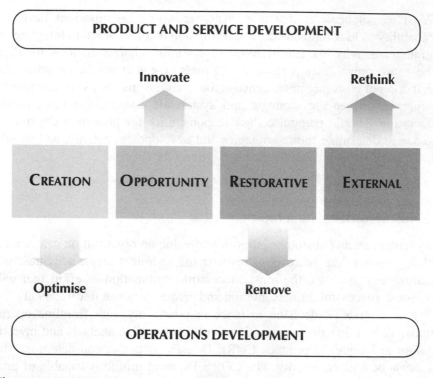

Figure 10.2 CORE operational development

CORE Demand organisational flow

CORE Demand data provides a measurement of performance for individual functions. For each function it is no longer appropriate to focus on functional targets: what is needed instead is a measurement of that function's capability to improve customer value and to remove organisational waste. Departments begin to determine their own strategic plans and development activities, based on customer intelligence as presented by frontline operations.

Again, if this is to happen the organisation must first take a strategic decision to allow operations to provide the intelligence that will determine organisational transformation (Figure 10.3). Examples of such transformation include appropriate recruitment principles, the nature of staff training, deployment of appropriate skilled resources, commercial agreements that promote shared value creation, technology that captures the nature of customer demand, and product teams who can produce new services in response to established demand.

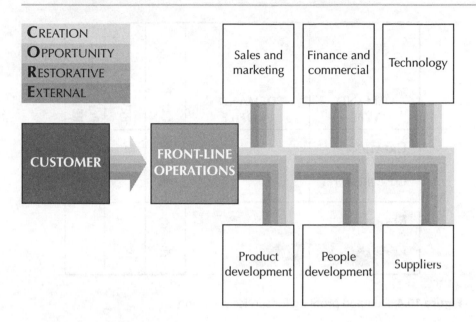

Figure 10.3 CORE Demand organisational flow

Some organisations go one stage further and make a strategic decision to use customer and CORE intelligence data to provide a view of the organisation's overall performance and success, as part of their balanced scorecard approach.

Demand profiling for service provision

As Figure 10.4 shows, if the organisation can profile customer demand it is possible to determine current performance and to predict future performance. This will illustrate how much time, effort and cost are already committed. Furthermore, latent opportunities can be identified, as well as important development activity.

Organisations that *do* place the strategic direction with operations can create an environment with many benefits: the removal of damaging hierarchies and 'silos'; the designing out of corporate waste; the creation of change based on customer data, not opinions; an environment that embraces customer variety and opportunity; and the alignment of end-to-end systems and processes to deliver against customer purpose and to create customer success.

DEMAND TYPE	DEMAND PROFILE	COST	REVENUE	POTENTIAL REVENUE
CREATION		€	€	
OPPORTUNITY		€		€
RESTORATIVE		€		
EXTERNAL		€	€	€

Figure 10.4 Demand profiling for service provision

Financial and commercial practices

This section is concerned with financial and accounting practices which support the establishment of a highly customer responsive organisation. A full discussion of financial controls and concepts is beyond the scope of this book, but other publications, including *Beyond Budgeting: How Managers can Break Free from the Annual Performance Trap* by Jeremy Hope and Robin Frazer (2003), and *Profit Beyond Measure* by H. Thomas Johnson and Anders Bröms (2001), cover the issues thoroughly. We will draw heavily on some of their insights.

New financial models

> Budgeting as practiced by most corporations should be abolished
>
> Hope and Frazer (2003)

> The budget is the bane of corporate America. It never should have existed. Making a budget is an exercise in minimalisation. You're always getting the lowest out of people, because everyone is negotiating to get the lowest number.
>
> Jack Welch, CEO of General Electric
> (in Hope and Frazer, 2003)

Changes to financial structures cannot be approached by stealth: there needs to be a clear, thought-through strategy, and communication based on customer demand CORE data.

Many good organisational change initiatives have fallen by the wayside because the financial models have not changed. In many cases we have seen clear benefits being delivered both to the end-to-end organisation and to customers, yet due to old functional models and budgets the benefits were not realised on the companies' bottom lines. The reason for this is simple: it is very difficult to persuade a functional cost-controller that in some cases maintaining or even increasing your local costs will reduce end-to-end cycle times and costs, and that this in turn will deliver better results to the organisation and customers. It is especially hard to make this case when the benefits will be realised in another department!

Traditional financial performance reports usually contain only lagging indicators. The problem with the budgeting process is that managers, in order to demonstrate that they have control, produce forecasts in order to be seen to *meet* their forecasts. Inherently they turn each 'forecast' into a commitment.

> Traditional budgeting sets not only a ceiling on costs but also a floor. It promotes centralisation of decisions and responsibility, makes financial control an annual Autumn event, absorbs significant resources across the organisation, and acts as a barrier to customer responsiveness.
>
> Bjartes Bognses, VP Corporate Control, Borealis
> (in Hope and Frazer, 2003)

Trying to ascertain what is happening in the business from budgeting information alone is like trying to play tennis by looking at the scoreboard. Even when investigations are initiated in order to understand the context in which the business was performing, the data and the knowledge will have been long lost. Managers then turn to speculation and 'in my experience' statements in order to demonstrate some sort of control.

The budget process usually creates the illusion that it is possible to focus on fixed targets around volume, revenue, profit and the like, whereas in reality it is simply reckless to focus on fixed targets and planning divorced from the dynamic context of business and the customer environment.

The functional financial model is supported by reporting systems and IT, which creates the illusion that by adding the parts together we will understand the whole. Even drilling deeper into the data will not always provide the answer – however seductive the information, the context or the customer intelligence might look, unless captured at the relevant time, will be difficult to reconstruct. We are reminded of the fossil hunter who drills down to remove the fossil and fails to take note of the surrounding clues about the environment in which the animal lived.

In many cases such financial reports can be contradictory to operational reports. This then sets in motion a hive of activity directed at rationalising the difference and demonstrating that the managers have maintained control. None of this activity creates value for customers. Many of the variances are in fact due to normal fluctuations in the business environment, which are impossible to predict. To maintain the illusion of control, however, managers must represent even these fluctuations as predictable.

The sum of the individual budgets does not make a cohesive whole, and trying to manage the organisation as if it consisted of individual independent parts is an approach that has outlived its usefulness. Edwards Deming, statistician and management innovator, believed that if management set quantitative targets and made people's jobs dependent on meeting them, 'they will likely meet the targets, even if they have to destroy the enterprise to do it'.

The effort required to manage budgets can take in excess of 35 per cent of managers' time. Budgeting practices are typically inflexible and backward-looking, and create a drag anchor even to *traditional* change. The move to an *on-demand* structure within operations therefore needs to be supported by a framework that moves from functional controls to end-to-end controls focused on different customer service demand types. In practice, this is not dissimilar to the product-line accounting found in lean manufacturing.

Process management

Many schemes and systems are used to manage, control and improve processes. The level of sophistication and complexity of process management usually reflects the complexity and diversity of the products and services being produced.

Process management principles

The following principles are a subset of the main principles outlined in the Re-Mind part of this book. Adhering to these principles will ensure that, whatever professional process management system has been implemented, evolution will be towards creating an on-demand organisation in which value flows continuously.

These principles do not replace the need for other support practices, such as change management, risk management, and training, but the fundamental objectives are to enable the staff who work within the process to measure their own work from the customers' perspective and to be free to experiment, in controlled conditions, with new approaches which they believe may improve the end-to-end measurement.

Our recommended process management principles are these:

1   Every process must support the creation of value as specified by the customer.
2   Process measurement needs be end-to-end, not functional.
3   Process change must be synchronised to customer need.
4   Those who work within the process should collect, analyse and act on customer data to improve the process.
5   Processes must promote continuous flow.
6   Processes must facilitate on-demand response to meet customer needs.
7   Test; improve; then document.
8   Engage in the relentless elimination of corporate waste.

Investigating and experimenting

Time spent by customer-facing staff in carrying out investigations, measurements, reflection and prototyping is often seen as unproductive time. However, staying in the line of fire and continuously processing work that creates no actual value is also unproductive.

Planned prototyping and experimentation uses the end-to-end capability measurements as a starting point to investigate the causes of performance variation. Here's a hypothetical example. Suppose that the capability to deliver goods on time is said to be 55 per cent: this figure is only the *mean*, however, and the important information is the *range*, which may vary between 45 and 85 per cent. Therefore the capability of the organisation – its ability to take an order and to deliver it on time – is thus reliably and predictably between 45 per cent and 85 per cent. On closer examination, it might be found that each customer request is causing a mini-crisis, and that each request gets handled in a different way: not because people will not follow the process guidelines, but because the processes are not equipped to deal with the variety of customer demands being made on the system. In such circumstances, staff usually shoehorn demand into inappropriate processes in an effort to provide the customer with at least *some* sort of service. All of this leads to internal wrangling, re-working, the expenditure of energy, and the amplification of demand because the customer has to try again.

The investigation into the *causes* of variation would look for the following characteristics:

1   Parameters that are due to external special causes, such as weather conditions, which do not affect the system's capability and for which redesign may be unnecessary.
2   Parameters that have a significant influence on performance, such as batch-and-queue design (the most common) and any inappropriate waste demand types that enter the system (in which case it is important to remove them rather than improve the system that deals with them).
3   Parameters that have no significance on performance – it is vital to *validate* assumptions about end-to-end performance.
4   Design parameters that could reduce the *cost* of service delivery without reducing the *capability* for service delivery.

Implementing improvements

Having tested a new process and determined that its impact on the end-to-end measurement is positive, adoption by the process management documentation system should be swift. A difficulty here is that insistence on adhering to previous processes in order to maintain audit compliance may be used as an excuse to keep things the way they are. In these circumstances the process management system becomes self-defeating, creating static processes and disengaging the staff who work within the process.

In many cases the over-complicated process management framework is in itself a source of great waste, as is evidenced by the large number of process manuals that just gather dust or the many defined processes that are not actually followed unless there is an audit. This therefore represents another form of pretence.

The process management framework must encourage changes continuously in pursuit of customer value creation – it simply cannot be true to say that the processes are perfect 'because they comply with audit standards'. *Processes are perfect when they optimally create value for customers.*

PART VI

Providing customer value

CHAPTER 11

Customer Value Enterprise®

Implementing a Customer Value Enterprise® strategy

Strategy and governance issues

> A company's capability to create value depends on its ability to implement strategies that respond to market opportunities by exploiting their internal resources and capabilities
>
> Penrose (1959)

Most organisations have difficulty in maintaining the links between corporate strategy and operational activities – the strategies can seem remote, even alien, to those who actually have to execute them. A clear line of sight is needed such that frontline workers on the ground can see from an operational perspective how to execute the high-level strategy. Yet while 'experts' at the top are looking at market trends and predicting the future, frontline staff are engaged in daily conversations in which they try to deliver today's customer needs while battling with management goals.

All too often, the top part of the organisation is gathering marketing intelligence and dealing with market positioning, while the frontline operation is dealing with actual customers and gathering customer intelligence. In contrast, a Customer Value Enterprise® organisation that chooses to pay attention to customer context and that systematically collects customer intelligence will obviously be in a better position to make informed decisions about any challenges it faces. In addition, the organisation's workforce will understand new market-positioning strategies and know how to realign the organisation quickly in response to these strategies. All work is a process – *strategy execution* is simply day-to-day work with a particular purpose in mind.

Most organisations treat strategy planning in the same way that they treat budget planning: as a one-off yearly function. For a Customer Value Enterprise®, however, strategy is iterative. No longer the preserve of an elite few at the top of an organisation, day-to-day strategy is developed by attuning corporate leaders to feedback from frontline staff about the real needs of customers. Frontline staff are seen by corporate leaders as a source

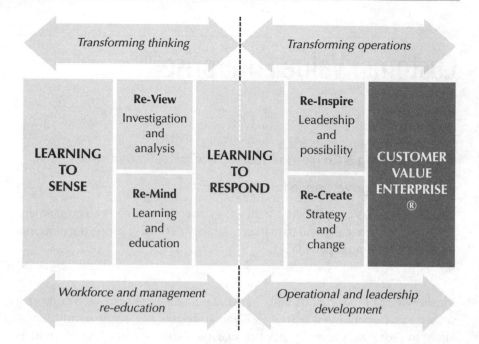

Figure 11.1 The Journey to Customer Purpose: Customer Value Enterprise®

of valuable input; the leaders are as ready to listen as to speak, and the organisation is designed and operated to encourage this important exchange of information. This is a world-beating combination – it not only applauds good strategies and strategists, but builds into the organisation the operational realignment and performance that will turn the strategy into practical day-to-day execution.

Strategy issues

Here are some of the typical difficulties experienced by organisations as they try to improve their performance:

- Strategies – where they exist – are not joined up.
- There are few links between lower-level activities and the broader goals.
- Because of a silo mentality, capability innovations are not shared – the wheel is continually reinvented.
- Communication is inconsistent.
- Accountability is questionable.

- Success is unpredictable.
- It is difficult to implement or change strategies quickly.
- It is difficult to interface strategies and to work across the business.
- It is slow and difficult to introduce new products and services.

In order to understand how an organisation's capabilities combine to create value, Robert S. Kaplan and David P. Norton, writing in *The Strategy-Focused Organisation* (2001), suggest the creation of visualisation maps that demonstrate the causal relationships between operations and strategy. They recommend a balanced scorecard approach:

> A strategy map for a Balanced Scorecard makes explicit the strategy's hypothesis. Each measure of a Balanced Scorecard becomes embedded in a chain of cause-and-effect logic that connects the desired outcomes from the strategy with the drivers that will lead to the strategic outcomes. The strategy map describes the process for transforming intangible assets into tangible customer and financial outcomes. It provides executives with a framework for describing and managing strategy in a knowledge economy.

Our approach is not to replace the Balanced Scorecard, but rather to ensure that knowledge derived from customer intelligence data is used to inform strategy and product development. An organisation moving towards an on-demand pull structure needs to make sure that demand management features within the strategy and governance models.

Organisational and management specification

As an organisation seeks to improve its own effectiveness, it needs a specification against which to build a strategy execution and operational development model. This model must:

- help develop the organisation's purpose and direction
- be scalable and consistent
- work at local capability and regional levels
- enable the prioritisation of strategic goals
- foster the co-ordination of diverse capabilities
- aid the introduction of best practice
- assist in capturing and reusing innovations
- promote the optimisation of capability performance
- support staff communication, inspiration and motivation
- be simple (but not simplistic) and acceptable
- provide a mechanism for unifying capabilities.

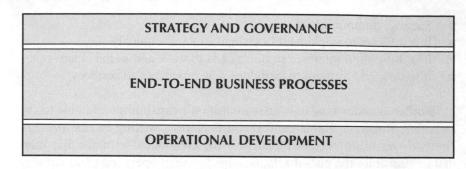

Figure 11.2 Customer Value Enterprise®: structure

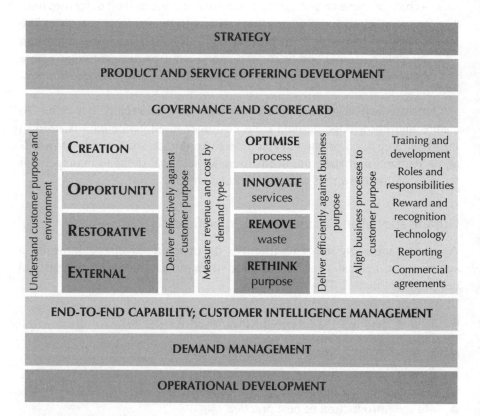

Figure 11.3 Customer Value Enterprise®: detail

Achieving an end-to-end Customer Value Enterprise®

Organisations need to connect business processes with the customer and with organisational strategy, and to step into a new role of managing demand profiles on the journey to creating a 'pull' service. Each element previously described – demand management, strategy development, customer intelligence, process management, end-to-end measurement, and governance – must now be seen in relationship to all the others. When each of these components is designed against Customer Value Principles, what emerges is an enterprise in which everything is judged against the creation of customer value: a *Customer Value Enterprise®*.

Contained within the model (Figure 11.3) can be seen the CORE Demand types and the operational response characteristics – optimise, innovate, remove, rethink – all aligned to business processes. End-to-end business process capability measurements are represented; they position the responsibility for optimisation of value and the removal of waste with delivery operations. Governance and strategy remain a central responsibility, but they can now take into account additional information derived from customer intelligence from frontline staff about potential services and markets that could be opened up. This arrangement clearly demonstrates corporate objectives and operational capability, while ensuring that the organisation makes the most of gathered intelligence.

In the next two chapters, case studies of two companies show clear evidence of how dramatically the end-to-end process affects living and breathing organisations. As you read them, consider the earlier list of strategy issues and how differently they are experienced in a true Customer Value Enterprise®.

CHAPTER 12

Abridged case study 1:
Office Products Direct Europe

This abridged case study, like that in Chapter 13, features a real example of the principles outlined in this book being applied to a company. (We have changed the name of the company and the people involved.) This study highlights only the pertinent points that reinforce those principles, and does not feature the plethora of tasks that are performed in any extensive transformation. Where necessary, we have adapted the language for the purposes of clarity. The study demonstrates how focusing on customer purpose can turn around a company when the situation is tough.

The case for change: a European company

This case study relates to operational change and transformation.

In the mid 1990s Office Products Corp. set up a network of superstores across Europe specialising in office equipment and supplies. The product range contained over 7000 items – a complex set of products, many of which needed specialist knowledge. In order to leverage the superstore network, Office Products Corp. USA decided to create Office Products Direct Europe, a direct-marketing catalogue business. The direct-marketing approach had been successfully established in the United States several years previously.

The European operation consisted of a large telesales centre, responsible for taking catalogue orders and running outbound telesales campaigns: they also dealt with after-sales enquiries and complaints. There were a number of warehouse locations where staff were responsible for the picking and packing of consignments. The supplier manager at each warehouse was responsible for managing the external distribution company that picked up the goods from that warehouse, ready for next-day delivery to customers.

The first two years of Office Products Direct Europe were very successful; the operation was growing steadily, meeting sales forecasts, and increasing the sales volume. It started to make profits and to gain market share. The early European growth cycle mirrored that seen in the USA. But this was very

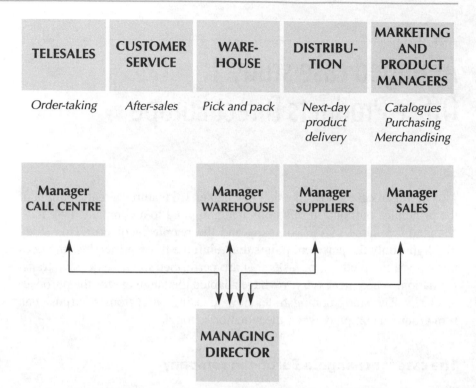

Figure 12.1 Case study: Office Products Direct UK

short-lived. High expectations were dashed as sales failed to materialise and operational controls failed to stabilise the situation. Anna King was brought in to recover the operation.

Anna King, Operations Director of Office Products Direct Europe, describes what happened when they embarked on the Journey to Customer Purpose:

> It is true to say that some conventional mass-production approaches would have produced some of these results but not all – the extent of the change, the speed and in particular those who influenced the change, i.e. the staff not only the managers, would have been very different. In addition, this approach has created a learning adaptive organisation which is now capable of meeting not only today's needs and solving acute operational problems, but it is now capable of dealing much more effectively with whatever changes it is called upon to perform in the future. In short we have created an organisation that is capable of understanding changing customer needs and adapting the organisation in response. This provides a long-term competitive advantage.

The most important lessons and findings were that the very design of the organisation was inhibiting sales growth and our ability to serve the customer. We also learnt how to identify good customer measurements, and how to align the organisation to what is important. We discovered an innovative customer-centric design and how to implement it. We found that organisational behaviour changed completely when the customer was put at the heart of the operation.

The reason we chose this approach was because we needed both to solve the immediate acute problems and to create an adaptive model for the future based on utilising the intelligence, ingenuity and creativity of all our staff.

I was tasked with creating a European-wide direct marketing service and to create a consistent approach across our European business.

In the UK operation, a business that was taking about 500,000 incoming sales orders per year generating about £9 million in sales revenue, I inherited a situation that can best be described as 'operational meltdown'. We had high operational costs, a broken-down infrastructure, low motivation and a complete failure to meet both customers' expectations and sales targets.

I looked at what the internal measures and reports might tell us, i.e. marketing, merchandising, telesales centre and distribution centres. We found that all internal targets other than profit were being met, yet the business was clearly in a dreadful state. It was obvious that any recovery in the UK would need a great deal of effort.

Transformation to a Customer Value Enterprise®

Here is an account of the transformation of Office Products Direct Europe into a Customer Value Enterprise®, in Anna King's own words.

Issues to be addressed

The company had experienced numerous difficulties: sales targets were not being met, and customer complaints and product returns were at an all-time high. Previous attempts to improve the situation resulted in the distribution company being changed, but customers still experienced delivery delays. As a result, goodwill compensation payments to disgruntled customers had risen, costing the company even more. Customers, tracking their orders and complaining about products and services, inundated the business with calls. These calls outnumbered sales calls 2:1.

As a result, over 18 per cent of customers hung up before speaking to a staff member, because waiting times were long. The overall working conditions worsened and staff turnover peaked at 40 per cent.

The problem is over there

Each function was only worried about its part in the process, and no one measured or even looked at end-to-end service delivery. The telesales staff accused marketing of withholding information about catalogue drops. The delivery issues were blamed on the distribution centre and the complaints department were inundated with re-delivery requests. Product line managers were blaming the sales staff for not selling hard enough. There were several members of staff constantly under-performing and there were high levels of absenteeism. We had extremely low morale, coupled with a strong feeling of futility. We took a two-week snapshot and found over 1600 serious customer service problems had been recorded, many of which resulted in compensation being given, in addition to refunds or replacement goods. We were losing more customers than we were gaining. And very worryingly, we had a significant amount of stock unaccounted for.

The operation had many broken and inefficient processes; there was little in the way of accurate information gathering and corrective action-taking. However, operations were recording just about all activity on a just-in-case basis.

It was chaotic, to say the least. I needed some data to understand what was really going on and where to start. I said to my senior management team, 'OK, we need to create an investigation team – we can't just blindly start changing things, we need to make sure the changes we make are the right changes. We don't have time to waste – it's make or break.'

Re-View

Team set-up and training

We formed a cross-functional, cross-hierarchical team who were going to investigate what customers really wanted. We introduced a new way to design, build and operate the business, and looked at ways to understand how functions interacted. This involved training the team to diagnose our operation from an outside-in perspective, identifying customer needs, applying customer-facing measures, identifying CORE Demand types and then measuring our end-to-end response capability. This would then provide us with a current state analysis and data upon which we would base our rescue plans.

When you select people for the investigation team, they need to be credible to the other parts of the organisation, because they will eventually lead the change and drive it home.

The team started looking at how we worked, doing what I call 'digging the process up', and came up with a large end-to-end system-performance map. They identified the waste, where we were repeatedly redoing things, and we were amazed to find double and triple data-entry.

The team also identified what measures were currently in place, and how people behaved in response to them. Within the telesales environment alone there were fifteen individual measures and, incredibly, not one focused on quality improvement or on customer service. All the measures were related either to staff resourcing or the number of sales, in one way or another, the intention being maximisation of staff availability and sales-order capture.

In reality, the functional way in which these measures were applied actually increased overall operating costs and resulted in massive customer dissatisfaction, as we will see later.

The investigation team surveyed our customers and started understanding what they really needed from us. They also sat down with their colleagues and started to understand the nature of CORE Demand and to determine the root causes and root costs.

We also asked the customers what was important to them. As you can see, it turned out to be really simple, and some would say obvious; many managers already knew this, but I have to ask myself the question, 'If it's so simple, obvious and important, then what prevented them from measuring it?' The answer was they thought that someone else would look after it, and if they all met their local goals and targets they assumed the customer needs would be satisfied. It was also perceived to be difficult to own and goal because some of the measures went across functional boundaries.

Items that were important to customers

Items that were important to customers:

1   Meeting our committed delivery time.
2   Accurate orders.
3   Good-quality products.
4   Advertised items being in stock.

So we decided: if these things are important to our customers, perhaps they should be important to us. We then introduced the purpose measures and tried to find out how we performed against them. The answer we got was not very encouraging, but at least we knew and could take action.

Current performance

We had a customer promise, 'guaranteed next-day delivery', but it was not measured. We decided to take a look at how we were actually performing against our commitment.

We sampled 200 orders per day from the previous six months, using control charts and statistical process-control methods. In March, for example, 'Committed delivery time' had a mean figure of 68 per cent, with a possible variation between 57 and 80 per cent. At this point we had no idea why it was so bad, but we knew that unless the process changed in some way, we could expect the mean and range to remain constant. Similar procedures were applied to establish the other measures.

- Committed delivery time   68 per cent
- Order accuracy   60 per cent
- Product quality   63 per cent
- In-stock items   67 per cent

The order accuracy was a known problem, yet nothing had been done about rectifying it. At least we now had a measure of how we were really performing.

We were amazed to find the number of items returned due to bad quality, all of which impacted our reputation and increased our recovery costs.

The stock level was very poor. If an item is out of stock in a store, the customer can walk around and look for something else: if you are out of stock in a catalogue business, then you're immediately into selling over the phone. So now the telesales assistant had to describe substitute products making 'up-sells' and 'cross-sells' very difficult.

Demand analysis

The team analysed in detail the nature of the requests being placed on the organisation. What they found was that 66 per cent of the incoming demand was restorative – 66 per cent of the incoming service requests were a direct result of something our organisation failed to do correctly.

Customer demand breakdown:

- C = 30 per cent
- O = 1 per cent
- R = 66 per cent
- E = 3 per cent

They also started to understand the things that resulted in service variation.

Walking the flow and identifying the causes of variation

In order to understand how the work flowed end-to-end through the organisation from taking the order to final delivery, we simply walked and mapped the flow.

While visiting the distribution centre, the team noticed a number of damaged products and asked the distribution supervisor if this was normal. According to the supervisor, products were damaged frequently because of inadequate packaging. Although the supervisor had informed the manager at the distribution centre, the distribution manager had not communicated this to the warehouse where the goods were packed. The team then went to the warehouse and spoke to the manager about the poor packaging. In order to reduce cost, the manager explained, the warehouse had begun to use cheaper materials but were unaware of the problems this had caused.

During the visit to the warehouse they made another discovery. While the label with the customer's name and mailing address was placed conspicuously on the outside of the box, any special delivery instructions were being packed inside along with the merchandise. Without these instructions, the distribution company could not, for example, deliver the goods in a certain window of time or leave them with a next-door neighbour. This resulted in a large number of customer complaints. By walking the flow, they identified many areas where errors and waste could simply be designed out.

Further examples:

- Product substitution lists were inaccurate.
- Postcode finder was five years out of date.
- Order entry system was slow.
- Customer invoices had errors.
- Warehouse computers were unable to reprint orders after printer jams, and the order was lost.

The issues seemed endless. However, having come up with an extensive list of things thought to be causing variation in service, we were confronted with a problem: how did we know if they were real issues or just a reflection of our own opinions? So we initiated some internal market research.

Quite simply the team put their findings into a questionnaire and asked everyone to express their opinions, stating if they agreed or disagreed, and asked if there were other issues the team had missed.

This had a number of benefits. First, it was validating the findings of the investigation team while gathering additional information; secondly, and perhaps more importantly, it provided a means of communication to the wider organisation, providing colleagues of the investigation team with a sense of what they were really up to and demonstrating the wide-ranging scope of the investigation.

We also conducted a survey about what managers thought was important and what took up most of their time. We also looked at how the current measuring system impacted the role of the manager, and what they were forced to pay attention to.

So now we had identified what matters to customers. We had made the system map with lots of highlighted waste, indicating problem areas, repeat data entry and so forth. Having completed the current-state analysis, it was time to share the information with the rest of the organisation – and it was not going to like what we had found.

Re-Mind

Managers joining up the dots for the first time

While the investigation team were completing their analysis, the rest of the management team were being put through some training and reorientation on Systems Thinking, leadership principles, Lean Service and statistical analysis techniques. We used case studies from previous companies who adhered to the mass-production ethos.

The funny thing is the managers said they would never do those sorts of things: 'Oh that's not us, we never do that, that's crazy.' However, when we later showed them the findings of the investigation team, supported with end-to-end data, there was a stunned silence. This is a very critical point in the transformation process: getting a view of reality, a compelling case for people to change what they are doing and paying attention to. As managers working from a functional mass-production perspective, they realise that what they've been doing has been detrimental to the operation, employees and customers, and that's quite a tough place to be. So the role of a senior leader is to create an environment where managers feel fairly secure in saying, 'Yes, I did that. Yes, I see it really needs to change.'

If you have a manager that comes from a typical command-and-control environment, and having taken them through the learning experience they just don't get it, you have to make a hard business decision and tell them this is no longer for them and 'We need to part company.' Unless you get your middle and higher managers to accept the current state without denial or defensiveness, you cannot make the changes necessary for sustained improvement.

Re-Inspire

For some staff involved in the investigation this was their first opportunity to understand the end-to-end process and interview managers. In order to feel confident to present their findings to management and other departments, a great deal of initial scepticism needed to dissipate, to be replaced with a self-confidence and the knowledge that they had gathered enough information to make recommendations. For some, even making an appointment to speak to a senior manager was an ordeal. Coaching and mentoring through these personal challenges built up staff courage and optimism.

Re-Create

In order to co-ordinate and structure the many changes we now needed to carry out, we created an 'Enterprise' plan. This was basically a change management structure that allowed us to track changes, gain agreement and resources, and demonstrate progress to the Board.

The managers and staff were working on the process not just within their function – they were using end-to-end measures and going to other functions and saying: 'I think we've got a problem here.' All those inter-departmental barriers fell down.

Performance management

Our performance was clearly linked to driving the four customer measures to change the CORE Demand profile. All departments were given these as strategic objectives. In addition to cross-functional objectives, there were team and individual objectives which had a clear linkage to the end-to-end measures. The reward and recognition system focused on people creating delivery capability, rather than driving output.

Job roles and structures

Originally, the telesales environment staffing levels were determined with Staffmax software. This had a fatal flaw in that it relied on previous call history profiles and did not take into account the differing nature of customer demand.

The old approach was to forecast, and to measure staff and managers on adherence to schedule. In reality the schedule did not reflect the changing nature of customer needs or demand profile: staff would attempt to adjust to the change in demand and fall foul of the adherence measures.

They learned to adhere to the schedule, which increased call-backs and complaints. The call-back demand was then incorporated into the Staffmax forecasting, which prompted managers to ask for more staff, based on the forecast model.

It was clearly evident that the staffing programme was causing disruption to the customer, loss of sales, increasing demand for headcount, and increased handling costs.

A new organisational design was devised, based on team cells. The objective of the new organisational design is to provide the telesales centre with staff that can be reassigned work at a moment's notice, responding to the incoming demand.

Customer Response Units

Each Customer Response Unit (CRU) has a telesales manager who manages between 25–30 staff. Staff are able to perform various customer added-value roles, and their pay is based on the value they can add to the customer. It is the manager's role, together with the team, to determine what roles each member would perform that day. Each role builds on the role before, e.g. to be qualified to carry out the coaching job you need to be qualified in telesales and operational response. You may be asked to perform any of these roles at any time.

Customer Response Units:

- Telesales — Takes sales orders.
- Operational Response — Customer service issues, low-level escalations.
- Coaching and Mentoring — Trainer (will prepare and deliver training).
- Process Improvement — CORE data and customer measure analysis.
- Telesales Manager — Manages the team.

The new CRU structure allows for job-enrichment and development, and increases the variety of tasks a team member can perform. This had a positive impact on employee retention, cost-reduction and customer service. More importantly, frontline staff designed the way that they do the work because they now felt a huge degree of ownership.

CRU benefits

- Clear sense of purpose.
- Trained staff to handle high-level problems and coach new staff.
- Reduced part-time staff.
- Improved job satisfaction.
- Employee retention.
- Career paths.
- Co-operative and collaborative approach to problem-solving.
- Fast prototyping of new solutions.
- Frontline staff learning and improving the system every day.
- Staff have responsibility to resolve issues in any part of the organisation.
- Focus is on demand and flow data, and less on individual performance.
- Establishment of a new team spirit.
- Reduced administration of daily staffing schedules.

In moving to the new structure we reduced the number of management layers, leaving a flatter organisation and quicker reporting lines.

Warehouse

The warehouse staff introduced cross-checking techniques for order accuracy, replaced warehousing software, rearranged layout to remove double-handling and reduce errors. An electronic manifest system was introduced between the warehouse and distribution, and all data was placed online for warehouse staff, telesales and the distribution company. New returns procedures were introduced which contributed greatly to reducing the time between order and billing. It also provided for better tracking of goods.

People development

People development focused on the acquisition of skills rather than moving departments. It was like promoting everyone. They got significantly improved job satisfaction, a lot more development; the customers were being served. However, we did lose some team members. There were some people who really could not work this way.

What we have seen within Office Products Direct is some tremendous personal development. There is a manager here now who was a frontline member of the investigation team; she's now one of the management team, possibly the fastest development into management that you've ever seen. She is totally capable of understanding this thinking; she knows what she's doing and there's a hoard of people following in her footsteps.

Sales and marketing

The sales team were responsible for developing business accounts. Due to improvements in customer satisfaction and customer access to more information, revenue from business clients increased.

Marketing used the knowledge of the telesales staff to test new product lines before inclusion in the catalogue; this was to reduce the incidents of poor-quality products being sold, and to provide early training on product features and benefits.

Process management

Office Products Direct did not have any procedures documented: this led to very haphazard and inconsistent ways of working. The investigation team processes were documented and this provided a comprehensive procedure manual. This became the source data for training and for determining new technology system requirements.

The first major thing we achieved was to change the order flow system, cutting out any waste which made it difficult for the customer to place an order.

Infrastructure

We now have a new IT system across finance, marketing, warehousing, telesales centre and merchandising.

The people who implemented it were mostly frontline staff from each department. Because they had gone through the earlier training, they knew what our system and customer requirements were. They were able to talk to the software developers and the installation technicians in a meaningful way. They also generated the training material to train their colleagues; and they also carried out the user-acceptance testing.

Staff were provided with access to the distribution company's website, which enables then to track orders, making sure they meet the committed delivery time.

This particular project – changing all the IT infrastructure including the network infrastructure – was the first project ever in Office Products Direct history that came in on time.

The results

We improved the committed delivery time to 95 per cent; the cost savings on this are significant. We save on extra delivery expense, compensation claims, time spent on the phone dealing with customer complaints; moreover we improve revenue, long-term, by satisfying more customers. It is difficult to put an exact figure on the savings, but a reasonable estimate of savings on compensation, delivery recovery expense and time spent on the phone is £15 per order.

The team clarified the purpose by implementing measures that tracked performance against end-to-end measures. They were free to experiment with new ideas and approaches. It became normal procedure for frontline staff to identify what processes were sub-optimised and where blockages and bad practices resulted in serious customer dissatisfaction.

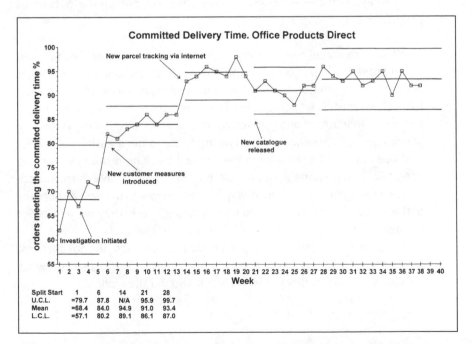

Figure 12.2 Case study: Office Products Direct UK – committed delivery time

Table 12.1 Case study: Office Products Direct UK – measurement results

Measurement	% Before	% After 9 months
Committed delivery time	68	95
Order accuracy	60	96
Quality of goods	63	85
In-stock levels	67	81

There were many significant improvements. For example:

■ 32 per cent reduction in restorative demand
■ 82 per cent reduction in customer complaints
■ 35 per cent reduction in order-entry time
■ 75 per cent reduction in compensation payments
■ business account registration reduced from four days to three minutes
■ increased stock availability
■ improved quality of packaging
■ discontinued poor-quality items
■ displayed customer's special delivery instructions on the outside of the box.

We also removed the customer complaints department, because we had improved our operational performance to a level where it was no longer required. Today the operation has more customer focus; the managers have a new 'customer' perspective. This was not process re-engineering – this was management and staff rethinking and then re-creating a new way of working, while subjugating everything to customer measures of value.

When I hear managers saying they have little or no resources to create operational improvement, I point out that they already have the resources but they are squandering them doing the wrong work. In this case 66 per cent of the resource was spent on doing the wrong work. They were in effect just institutionalising waste, locking in resources and costs.

Our people have had such an incredible journey, such brilliant personal development – we just showed people the information, focused on what the customers wanted, and they went out and did the work.

CHAPTER 13

Abridged case study 2: Fujitsu Services Ltd

This abridged case study, like that in Chapter 12, features a real example of the principles outlined in this book being applied to a company. The study only highlights the pertinent points that reinforce those principles, and does not feature the plethora of tasks that are performed in any extensive transformation.

Where necessary, we have adapted the language for the purposes of clarity.

The case for change: a global company

> [The lean] approach has been pursued brilliantly by Fujitsu Services.
>
> Womack and Jones (2005)

This case study outlines the introduction of a 'Sense and Respond' strategy into Fujitsu Services Ltd. It focuses on the work carried out in Fujitsu's IT service delivery environments.

Fujitsu Services Ltd is one of the leading IT services companies in Europe, the Middle East and Africa. It has an annual turnover of £1.74 billion (€2.58 billion), employs 14,500 people, and operates in more than twenty countries. It designs, builds and operates IT systems and services for customers in the financial services, telecoms, retail, utilities, and government markets. Its core strength is the delivery of IT infrastructure management and outsourcing across desktop, networking and data centre environments, together with a full range of related services from consulting through to integration and deployment.

Definition of terms

For clarity, in this case study the term *client* or *clients* will refer to corporations that contract with Fujitsu for its services. Fujitsu Services Ltd has contracts with over four hundred clients, many of which are household names. Furthermore, the service user will be referred to as the *customer* or *customers*, be they corporate employees or members of the general public.

Reasons to change, challenges in changing

Drivers for change:

- The need to differentiate to catch market leaders.
- The desire to achieve industry-leading levels of customer retention in an aggressive marketplace.

Challenges:

- To create shared services while delivering tailored services to diverse clients.
- To integrate helpdesks, mobile field engineering, and enterprise management.
- To improve project management co-ordination and implementation.
- To improve performance measurement, efficiency of service delivery, and the sharing of resources and of knowledge.
- To work with 22 service locations and over 400 corporate clients in the UK.
- To renew technology infrastructure.

Transformation

The action plan

- Transform organisational performance – thinking, learning and measurement.
- Educate the marketplace to have higher expectations.
- Create a new operating model that would differentiate Fujitsu Services Ltd from its competitors.
- Start in the UK and roll out worldwide.

Past and present

In 1999 there was a growing realisation at Fujitsu that the traditional approach to service needed to be overhauled if Fujitsu wanted to get an edge on the larger US service providers. Operating in the IT-outsourcing sector,

Fujitsu found itself in a very aggressive marketplace: to compete with its larger competitors, it needed to have a very strong differentiator. Many client accounts were under threat, and high levels of client satisfaction were needed to secure the customer base. Furthermore, the turnover of frontline call centre staff was 42 per cent, slightly above the industry average, and needed to be reduced.

Fujitsu Services serves many different customer groups across several industry sectors and has numerous customer entry points throughout the organisation. When analysis was carried out, Fujitsu found that 30–80 per cent of incoming service requests were entirely preventable. This level of waste was unnecessary, yet unavoidable under existing mass-production system constraints. This highlighted areas where Fujitsu could improve productivity and, more importantly, where it could improve client satisfaction. Fujitsu needed to look at what was creating *value* for customers and what was not. It became clear that if it could identify the causes of inefficiency and remove them at source, it could gradually decrease the time spent on value restoration and increase the time spent on value creation for the customer. This was an opportunity to change the way Fujitsu worked with its customers, and even to change its service offerings.

Following the implementation of 'Sense and Respond', Fujitsu encourages frontline staff to identify any problems, fix them, and take the necessary measures to prevent them from recurring. Fujitsu is fostering a new relationship between frontline staff and customers. Frontline employees are able to create new performance measurements based on purpose as defined by customers and the organisation: they then redesign their own work to meet both needs. Knowledge generated from this new perspective and driven by the frontline staff allows the rest of the organisation to redesign itself to meet the needs of its frontline staff and customers.

As well as a new relationship with customers, therefore, Fujitsu also promotes a different relationship between the frontline staff and the rest of the organisation. As shown in Figure 13.1, sensing and responding puts people at the centre. As a result, company-wide transformation has occurred from the bottom up and has cut across all departments, with customer knowledge ascending the command chain. This has changed the whole culture of the customer service organisation.

While the initial implementation took place in the helpdesk arena, Fujitsu soon recognised the potential of the 'Sense and Respond' strategy and applied it in a wider context. In addition to the helpdesk environment, these principles have now been applied to mobile engineering, human resource online services, the payroll, the supply chain, remote IT management, and pre-contract analysis.

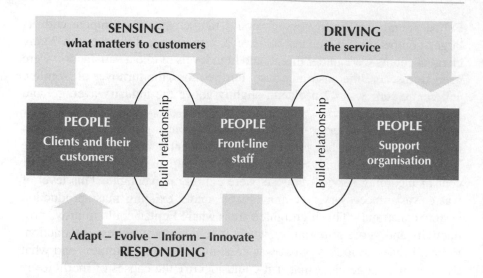

Figure 13.1 Case study: Fujitsu Services Ltd – people, people, people

Implementation

Fujitsu began to redesign its services, with a new emphasis on people, the problem-solving process, and value creation. This involved the identification of training needs, the deployment of new skills, and the reorganisation of roles and responsibilities. New key performance indicators and service-level agreements were built around the business goals and business rules of clients.

Implementation phases

The implementation phases of Fujitsu's new learning system were as follows.

- **Phase 1: Learning to *Sense***
  - View the organisation from a customer perspective.
  - Evaluate value-chain measurement horizontally and vertically.
  - Understand frontline roles and responsibilities.

- **Phase 2: Learning to *Respond***
  - Re-educate management.
  - Introduce the 'Pull' theory of management.
  - Replace 'make and sell' mass-production thinking with theories that incorporate Systems Thinking, Lean Production and Transformational Leadership.

- **Phase 3: Leading change**
  - Utilise Transformational Leadership theories.
  - Employ cognitive behaviour methodology.
  - Operate within a leadership and coaching framework.
  - Award staff and managers with accreditations.

- **Phase 4: Mobilising**
  - Create an organisation capable of *designing itself against customer demand* by implementing an operational framework focused on value creation.
  - Provide detailed change programmes to transform the corporate infrastructure.
  - Implement a business process management system, including a high-level measuring system for monitoring end-to-end business processes such as HR, training, commercial, product development, and technology.
  - Adopt transformational approaches and principles.
  - Design domestic and international plans for mobilisation.
  - Provide in-country support for operations.

The impact of implementation

Initially, eight hundred members of staff were trained. In essence, the hierarchy within Fujitsu was turned upside-down. The role of managers was changed from one of authority to one of support. Their central responsibility became the provision of the necessary knowledge and tools to allow frontline staff to handle the needs of the customer and to assume responsibility for the end-to-end service – even if that service left the confines of the helpdesk at Fujitsu and was transferred to other client suppliers.

In addition to outsourcing IT, Fujitsu also supplies IT helpdesk services to its own employees. It has:

- removed as much as 60 per cent of the incoming demand
- reduced service operating costs by 64 per cent
- improved advisor productivity by 45 per cent
- reduced end-to-end cycle time by 70 per cent
- increased user satisfaction by 30 per cent.

So successful has this been that Fujitsu has recently taken its UK-developed model and deployed it into operations in South Africa, Australia, Finland, Netherlands, and Japan.

Fujitsu Services Ltd is now able to offer many clients reduced annual costs, because it is confident about removing preventable demand. This approach has positively impacted customer and client satisfaction, employee satisfaction and operating costs. Commercial contracts between Fujitsu Services Ltd and its clients had to be restructured to realise mutual benefit from call reduction and reduced remedial activities. Many clients are now charged *for each potential user* of the service, not for the number of service requests actually placed or IT devices fixed. This gives Fujitsu a strong incentive to remove the causes of failure within the IT infrastructure, as company profits are directly related to the reduction of infrastructure failure and client business outcomes.

The results

With a 'Sense and Respond' strategy, Fujitsu Services Ltd has had the following results:

- customer satisfaction has increased by 28 per cent
- employee satisfaction has increased by 40 per cent
- staff attrition has decreased from 42 per cent to 8 per cent
- operating costs have been reduced by 20 per cent
- contract renewal and service upgrades have amounted to £200m.

Roles within the service are constantly changing in response to the proactive actions of the people within it. This creates a dynamic culture, and feedback from staff revealed that they are highly motivated and proud to be part of an innovative and creative organisation.

Feedback from staff

Staff were asked what difference the new way of working made to them. Some of their comments were as follows:

- '["Sense and Respond"] provided a total shift in my way of thinking, getting into the customer's business and absorbing it.'
- 'Putting the customer's needs first, every time. Getting rid of the waste and concentrating on delivering what matters.'
- '["Sense and Respond"] has allowed me to approach things from a different angle, look at the facts and disregard opinions and stories.'
- 'I can now present data and facts to show reality and be committed to providing opportunities for others.'

- 'I have become much calmer. I can see the impact I can make.'
- '["Sense and Respond"] has given me a much broader perspective and a new focus. I now see happy customers. I can now see what will make them happy.'
- 'I am learning what matters to my customers.'
- 'I discovered a new way of thinking for myself and about the role I perform, and that using relevant data can assist in changing people's attitudes.'

Response from customers

The implementation of a 'Sense and Respond' strategy at Fujitsu has had other effects:

- At Fujitsu itself, removing preventable service calls at the source has not resulted in the reduction of staff. Quite the opposite: Fujitsu's customers have responded by outsourcing more work to Fujitsu because they see the real value in doing so.
- Fujitsu has redesigned its activities not on market intelligence but on customer knowledge and end-to-end performance data. 'Sense and Respond' has become a major differentiator that distinguishes this company from its competitors in the eyes of its existing and potential customers.
- One leading Fujitsu client decided to share its IT infrastructure outsourcing between many suppliers, and initially awarded Fujitsu its helpdesk contract. Using a 'Sense and Respond' strategy, the Fujitsu helpdesk staff observed that 30 per cent of the incoming demand was a direct result of third parties failing to meet customer needs. When action was taken on this data, incoming calls were reduced by 24 per cent in one month. Fujitsu later went on to win the client's entire IT business.

The ripples from Fujitsu's innovations have spread outward, as some of Fujitsu's clients have embraced the approach themselves and have also begun to reap the benefits.

- One such is bmi, a European airline company. Acting on business and customer context intelligence, bmi has managed to reduce queues at ticket offices, check-ins and boarding gates. bmi CIO Richard Dawson stated 'Over the last two years, calls have been reduced by 40 per cent and time to fix reduced by 70 per cent.'

- A large government client has seen customer satisfaction ratings raised from 5.2 to 8.2, a 63 per cent increase.
- A training consultancy providing education and skills to adults reported an increase in customer satisfaction from 'acceptable' to 'highly satisfied' in the space of just four months. Additionally, the consultancy experienced:
  - first-contact fix (Fujitsu's own measurement of response to clients) increased by 64 per cent
  - end-to-end service cycle time reduced by 60 per cent
  - end-to-end service costs decreased by 30 per cent
  - value : preventable demand ratio moved from 10 : 90 to 60 : 40.

Industry recognition for 'Sense and Respond'

The *'Sense and Respond' strategy* has received both direct and indirect recognition.

- In 2001, Fujitsu was awarded the European Call Centre of the Year award for the Best People Development Programme.
- At the 2002 National Business Awards, Fujitsu were finalists in the Customer Focus Category.
- At the 2003 National Business Awards, 'Sense and Respond' was awarded Best Customer Service Strategy. The judges praised Fujitsu, saying that it had demonstrated an entire cultural change around the needs of its customers and could, as a result of its customer service strategy, demonstrate business growth, innovation and success.

> Through applying a 'Sense and Respond' strategy, Fujitsu has achieved remarkable mastery in the use of staff and client knowledge to drive continuous improvement. In particular, they have converted customer knowledge into powerful drivers of business strategy.
>
> Joel Cutcher-Gershenfeld, Senior Research Scientist,
> Engineering Systems Division and
> Sloan School of Management, MIT

Making the transformational journey

Reflections from a manager

Below are the reflections of a manager on her personal transformation journey. They illustrate the ups and downs of the experience of creating leadership in others, and of experiencing the profound impacts and benefits of this process.

> What I discovered and learnt from going through a Customer Value diagnosis for the first time as a manager was that the approach was not only about designing processes on new principles: it was fundamentally about the way people at different levels within the organisation think about the nature of work itself. It's also about creating leadership at all levels of the organisation. Not everyone wants to become a leader; and sometimes, where leadership has been absent, the initiatives have stalled. People discover the truth about how their behaviour is linked to operational performance. It provides a realistic picture of the entire system, how services are really delivered. It's about opening the door to change the future.
>
> Strong leadership, commitment, courage and a sheer dogged determination are required to see it through to the end. When people realise the cost of doing nothing, not only for the company but personally, they are inspired to carry out the difficult steps to change the systems in which they work. When people change their behaviour and influence their working environment it creates for me a moving and heartfelt pride.
>
> We carried out post and prior employee surveys with the following results [Table 13.1].
>
> When asked if employees felt they had sufficient authority to do their job well, it went from 76 per cent to 97 per cent where staff felt they could do their jobs without gaining approval from their managers.
>
> Customer satisfaction increased from 6 out of 10 to 9 out of 10, and the customer then proceeded to give our company their entire business to manage from other suppliers.
>
> The 'Sense and Respond' strategy had the greatest impact on transforming people into leaders. When people learn to use customer intelligence data to inform the rest of the organisation, there are no places to hide, the

Table 13.1 Case study: Fujitsu Services Ltd – employee survey

Question	Pre %	Post %
Is my working life not stressful?	60	72
Are you exceeding customer's expectations?	29	72
Do staff believe ideas are listened to?	50	80
Is the workforce motivated?	47	86
Do managers deliver on their promises?	61	86
Have you sufficient authority to do your job well?	76	97

moment of truth arrives, it becomes crunch time. To some people it's a shock but to others it just opens their eyes and makes them realise they have been keeping their heads down without questioning 'Is there a better way to do this?' The greatest revelation is the change in responsibilities where you would normally see the operations manager or service director directing the change, instead frontline staff become the agents for change as they fundamentally understand the customer transactions and with the gathered customer intelligence, are now listened to. The frontline becomes the greatest barometer of service performance – not a client director – a frontline person. In one situation I remember a frontline person being flown to the customer's headquarters to present information to the board of directors. The frontline employee was not familiar with board presentations but had acquired the courage, belief and the commitment to stand up and present the reality and data related to the customer environment and what was needed to create service improvement.

For managers who go through the experience it is sometimes frightening, especially when they want to keep the job they were doing. I realised, too, that I had to perform a completely different role: rather than dictating to my team, I sought advice from them. The manager takes on a supporting role and their responsibility is to enable the frontline person to create the levers for change. Traditional management focus is inwards and vertically downwards; that changed to outwards and horizontally across the functional boundaries.

For me to express my personal transformation, I don't know where to begin. It is an evolutionary journey for me. As a manager, it has totally changed the way I am; it allowed me to change the way that I work with my staff. It has taken the weight off my shoulders; it's allowed me to breathe and enabled me to become a leader and harness support from the network of leaders when needed. It was almost like making my job redundant, because from my perspective the frontline are capable of leading the change for themselves. I then moved to other operations and created new leaders elsewhere, so the transformational journey broadens into other parts of the business.

I have a greater role now to create leaders throughout the organisation and that's a big responsibility. It makes me ask the right questions, both personally and professionally – 'What is the purpose of the work I'm trying to do; what really matters; what is it I really need to achieve to meet purpose?' A 'Sense and Respond' strategy creates an opportunity for all people to do things differently: it creates leaders that can transcend the constraints and create a new culture.

CHAPTER 14

Customer purpose at the heart of the organisation

The journey of transformation

We have outlined a journey of transformation whereby organisations can become highly responsive to the needs of their customers and can become differentiated from their competitors by their ability to continually adapt, innovate and deliver customer success. Organisations generally regarded as leading business practice, which are challenging the boundaries of the conventional structures and changing decision-making patterns, are creating a new paradigm of customer-value service provision. They are making a stand, finding the courage to question what has gone before them, and interrogating how past practices have dictated the organisations' very existence. Organisations that embark on the journey to create a Customer Value Enterprise® need to recognise the tenacity, authenticity and courage it takes to systematically align the entire resources of the corporation to customer purpose. On the other hand, they may also recognise that it is precisely this journey towards customer alignment that will help to guard against their own commercial extinction.

Organisations that sense what's important to customers and that create the capability to respond to customer demand have instigated a new service strategy: when implemented, this puts the customer at the heart of the organisation. It creates a customer-knowledge-driven culture, based on Transformational Leadership, Customer Value Principles, and organisational diagnosis. This culture differentiates between activities that optimise customer value and activities that create corporate waste. It develops a customer-centric environment that puts strategy realisation at the frontline and embraces customer knowledge end-to-end, identifying barriers and creating new possibilities for an authentic business environment in which people have the choice, freedom and power to do what instinctively they already know matters.

Organisations embark on the four-stage journey – Re-View, Re-Mind, Re-Inspire and Re-Create – understanding that each component is highly

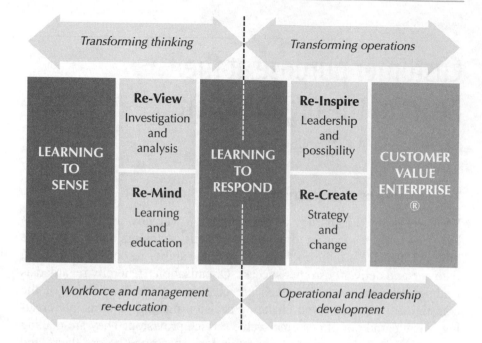

Figure 14.1 The Journey to Customer Purpose

interactive, and that no one part is ever completed but remains in a continual state of change, sensing and responding to the demands of the environment. That is the essence of profound transformation in highly adaptive organisations.

The journey begins by defining a view of current service provision through the eyes of the customer, and thereby reveals the true reality. The organisation chooses to recognise and respond to this reality: it identifies barriers to change, breaks through functional and organisational conflicts, and creates a service environment that recognises the areas most in need of attention and redesign.

It is only brave and aspirational companies that know they need to behave in this way – to do something different. It is only these same brave and aspirational companies that have the courage and integrity to take an authentic look at themselves through the eyes of the customer and not to lose focus, even if they are shocked by what they find. Looking through the eyes of customers, organisations learn to understand how their end-to-end structures operate as one system, and they begin to scrutinise all of the organisation's functions and activities in relation to customer purpose. Once they have diagnosed the *context* in which the customers transact with the service organisation, they can more fully understand the value that their service creates.

Managers and other staff may experience a reality shock when they come to realise not only that the organisation has been treating all demand the same, but the large and avoidable costs to the organisation of doing this. Having faced this, however, they can start to make a positive change. Often they will be able to invest resources differently in order to minimise the processing of wasteful and avoidable demand. As they go on gathering data and faithfully comprehending the reality, the Transformational Leaders may encounter highly guarded power structures and resistance to facing the facts of current service capability. They may discover safety nets that people have created for themselves, and recognise the personal discomfort for these people that is implicit in change.

The Transformational Leaders will recognise powerful and pervasive thought models conditioned by mass-production thinking. They will initiate the re-engineering of mental models, which is probably the most important aspect of organisational change – without such a change in thinking there can be no reconstruction. Their very approach presumes an organisation that has the right mindset to keep redesigning itself against the needs of the customer, and builds the foundations for Transformational Leaders who can later work beyond standards to touch, move and inspire others through conversations about what is *really* important.

Organisations that are capable of sensing what is important to customers require a new form of leadership: leadership that invites transformation, that welcomes reinvention, that espouses continuous metamorphosis over time. Such an organisation aims to define itself by the nature of incoming demand. The organisation's entire design, and the alignment of all the activities that support it, are dictated by the need to create a constant state of change in response to the flow of customer value.

The single factor that most clearly distinguishes the Customer Value Enterprise® and enables sustained organisational change is the institutionalised respect and acknowledgement of the intelligence, skills and insights of frontline staff, and the capacity to lead that exists at all levels within the organisation. All staff can understand and influence people's behaviour; all can recognise that the performance of the organisation is an outcome of the collective interactions between employees, departments and customers.

If the organisation is to move forward and create breakthrough results, it certainly needs a Customer Leadership Culture that will address any resistance to change. But resistance will not be overcome simply by management polemics: to embrace change, staff need to go through an experience that reveals to them the world as it is really seen by their colleagues and the customer. This experience will highlight the suffocating impacts of out-of-date principles and working practices, their damaging impacts on the well-being of staff, and the inevitable conflicts that arise in managing the customer relationship. Once individual employees conceive a new view of the future, coupled with the ability to express new possibilities clearly in conversation, taking into account their listener's own perspective, those individuals will have *power*. They will be able to inspire colleagues to take meaningful action and to create a working environment they had not imagined to be possible. Rather than waiting for change to happen and the environment to improve, these same people can step into positions of responsibility and *make* change happen. The most important work of the organisation is using the innate talent of staff who have conversations about the customer's world so that it can capture customer intelligence.

New relationships are developed with customers. These highlight the organisational freedoms that will allow improved service provision, reduced operating costs, increased profitability, and increased customer spending. These are relationships that foster honesty and openness about reality. Truly customer-centric organisations have the capability to lock on to customer purpose and to integrate all strategic activity with one common intent: to align the entire organisation's resources to meet customer needs, with a sustained focus on serving customers.

Characteristics of a true Customer Value Enterprise®

Is your organisation really on the way to becoming a Customer Value Enterprise®? Has it truly grasped the Customer Value Principles approach and made this into a core competency?

The words of G. Hamel and C. K. Prahalad in their book *Breakthrough Strategies for Seizing Control of Your Industry and Creating the Markets of Tomorrow* (1994) identify the principal characteristics of an organisation that embraces transformational change:

- The organisation has a flexible and responsive collective learning capacity.
- The organisation integrates multiple skills and technologies.
- The organisation has the capability to combine resources and knowledge to deliver superior products and services.
- The organisation has at least one differentiator that makes it competitive.
- The very fabric of the organisation is what sets it apart.
- The organisation's approach uniquely identifies it.
- The organisation's adaptability is difficult to copy.

- The organisation has a feel or quality that is difficult to articulate: rather than being one specific approach or strategy, success seems to be tied up in a combination of technologies, processes and 'just the way things are done around here'.

The biggest single distinguishing characteristic of a Customer Value Enterprise® is its organisational alignment to customer purpose, coupled with respect for the potential contribution of effort and insight of every member of staff. This approach has dramatic effects on the people who experience the Journey to Customer Purpose. We leave you with some truly inspiring comments from the people we have worked with – people in various organisations and at various levels in those organisations.

- 'I have my integrity back. I no longer have to lie.'
- 'It's opened up enormous possibilities for my other customers.'
- 'I am now a *leader* and an *enabler*.'
- 'I am excited, happy and fulfilled.'
- 'I listen more, I am motivated again. I want to change things; I can see a future.'
- 'It has changed my thinking.'
- 'I feel motivated in delivering a program that can have a huge impact on business, employees and customers.'
- 'It's been life-changing – literally.'
- 'It has helped me get rid of my past and remain present. It's given me a compass to follow from now on.'
- 'A better way of working, feeling comfortable with myself, getting out of the old "mindset". Being able to recognise the old way of working and helping others to have integrity and be inspired.'
- 'Possibilities can be created from data. Those possibilities can be achieved by people who have been inspired and have the courage to take responsibility and make choices.'
- 'A completely new outlook on not just work, but life!'
- 'I have also realised that I have been living a lie at work.'
- 'This is more than a management technique. It looks at business as one large, often diverse, but highly interrelated organism.'
- 'It is about aligning everything to add value to the customer's experience.'
- 'I learnt how to stop panicking, take a step back; and it's crystallised a lot of what I vaguely thought but wouldn't express – now I can express it.'

REFERENCES

- Beer, Stafford: *Diagnosing the System: for Organisations* (Wiley, 1994).
- Bosworth, Michael T. and John R. Holland: *Customer Centric Selling* (McGraw-Hill, 2004).
- Crainer, Stuart: *Key Management Ideas* (Financial Times Professional, 1998).
- Cutcher-Gershenfeld, Joel and Kevin Ford: *Valuable Disconnects in Organizational Learning Systems: Integrating Bold Visions and Harsh Realities* (Oxford University Press, 2005).
- Downey, Myles: *Effective Coaching* (Texere, 1999).
- Edwards Deming, W.: *Out of the Crisis* (1982: reprinted MIT Press, 2000).
- Einstein, Albert (1879–1955). Quoted from website: swamij.com/einstein.htm.
- Einstein Network: *The Business Channel* (Programme 1290, 2004).
- Fromm, Erich: *The Art of Being* (1950: reprinted Constable, 1992).
- Gharajedaghi, Jamshid: *Systems Thinking: Managing Chaos and Complexity* (Butterworth Heinemann, 1999).
- Goodwin, Brian: 'All for one … one for all', in *New Scientist*, vol. 2138 (June 1998).
- Haeckel, Stephan H.: *Adaptive Enterprise: Creating and Leading Sense and Respond Organizations* (Harvard Business School, 1999).
- Hamel, G. and C. K. Prahalad: *Breakthrough Strategies for Seizing Control of Your Industry and Creating the Markets of Tomorrow* (Harvard Business School, 1994).
- Hay, Louise L.: *You Can Heal Your Life* (Hay House UK Ltd, 1984).
- Holweg, Matthias and Frits K. Pil: *The Second Century: Reconnecting Customer and Value Chain through Build-to-Order* (MIT Press, 2004).
- Hope, Jeremy and Robin Frazer: *Beyond Budgeting: How Managers can Break Free from the Annual Performance Trap* (Harvard Business School, April 2003).
- Johnson, H. Thomas and Anders Bröms: *Profit Beyond Measure* (Free Press, November 2001).
- Kaplan, Robert S. and David P. Norton: *The Strategy-Focused Organisation* (Harvard Business School, 2001).
- Kasich, John: *Courage Contagious* (Main Street Books, 1999).
- Kotter, John P. and Dan S. Cohen: *The Heart of Change* (Harvard Business School, 2002).

- Landmark Education: www.landmarkforum.com (workshops on personal change).
- Lao Tzu: *The Art of War* (6th century BCE).
- Penrose, E. T.: *The Theory of the Growth of the Firm* (New York: John Wiley, 1959).
- Rother, Mike and John Shook: *Learning to See: Value Stream Mapping to Add Value and Eliminate Muda* (Lean Enterprise Institute, February 1999).
- Seddon, John: *I Want You to Cheat: The Unreasonable Guide to Service and Quality Organisations* (Vanguard, 1992).
- Shewhart, Walter A.: *Statistical Method: From the Viewpoint of Quality Control* (Dover, 1986).
- Taylor, Frederick Winslow: *The Principles of Scientific Management* (1911: reprinted).
- Taylor, P. and P. Bain: 'An assembly line in the head: work and employee relations in the call centre', in *Industrial Relations Journal* 30:2 (1999).
- Womack, James P. and Daniel T. Jones: *Lean Thinking: Banish Waste and Create Wealth in Your Corporation* (Simon & Schuster, 1996).
- Womack, James P. and Daniel T. Jones: 'Lean Consumption', in *Harvard Business Review* (March 2005).
- Womack, James P., Daniel T. Jones and Daniel Roos: *The Machine that Changed the World* (Rawson Associates, 1990).
- Wright Mills, C.: *Power Elite* (Oxford Press, 1956).
- Zander, Rosamund Stone and Benjamin Zander: *The Art of Possibility* (Harvard Business School, 2000).

This book has tried to explain a very large breadth of subject matter in a small amount of space. Readers who wish to explore particular topics in greater detail may find the following books and articles of interest.

The subjects range from popular business literature to technical research. The books have been grouped to match the four phases of the Journey to Customer Purpose. Many of these texts have been used in our own research and some have influenced our thinking over some time. The list also acknowledges the contribution of earlier thinkers to the body of knowledge contained in Systems Thinking, Lean Thinking, Leadership, Analytical Management Tools, and change.

Re-View

- Beer, Stafford: *Diagnosing the System: for Organisations* (Wiley, 1994).
- Bicheno, John: *The Lean Toolbox* (Picsie, 2000).
- de Bono, Edward: *Lateral Thinking for Management* (McGraw Hill, 1971).
- Kume, Hitoshi: *Statistical Methods for Quality Improvement* (Gilmour Drummond, 1987).
- Lareau, William: *Office Kaizen* (American Society for Quality, 2003).
- Oakland, John S.: *Total Quality Management* ([Heinemann Professional], 1989).
- Ross, Phillip J.: *Taguchi Techniques for Quality Engineering* (McGraw Hill, 1995).
- Seddon, John: *I Want You to Cheat: The Unreasonable Guide to Service and Quality Organisations* (Vanguard, 1992).
- Senge, Peter, Art Kleiner, Charlotte Roberts, Rick Ross and Bryan Smith: *The Fifth Discipline Fieldbook* (Nicholas Brealey, 1994).
- Shewhart, Walter A.: *Statistical Method: From the Viewpoint of Quality Control* (Dover, 1986).
- Wheeler, Donald J.: *Understanding Variation: the Key to Managing Chaos* (SPC Press, 2000).

Re-Mind

- Beer, Stafford: *The Brain of the Firm: Managerial Cybernetics of Organization* (Lane, 1972).

- Checkland, Peter: *Systems Thinking, Systems Practice* (Wiley, 1998).
- Edwards Deming, W.: *Out of the Crisis* (1982: reprinted MIT Press, 2000).
- Gleick, James: *Chaos: The Amazing Science of the Unpredictable* (Vintage, 1996).
- Johnson, H. Thomas and Anders Bröms: *Profit Beyond Measure* (Nicholas Brealey, 2000).
- Liker, Jeffrey: *The Toyota Way: Fourteen Management Principles from the World's Greatest Manufacturer* (McGraw-Hill, 2003).
- Ohno, Taiichi: *The Toyota Production System* (Productivity Press, 1978).
- Womack, James P. and Daniel T. Jones: *Lean Thinking: Banish Waste and Create Wealth in Your Corporation* (Simon & Schuster, 1996).
- Womack, James P., Daniel T. Jones and Daniel Roos: *The Machine that Changed the World* (Rawson Associates, 1990).

Re-Inspire

- Fromm, Erich: *Man for Himself: an Enquiry into the Psychology of Ethics* (Routledge, 2002 [based on a publication from 1950]).
- Maslow, Abraham: *Maslow on Management* (Wiley, 1998).
- Zander, Rosamund Stone and Benjamin Zander: *The Art of Possibility* (Harvard Business School, 2000).

Re-Create

- Cummings, Thomas and Christopher Worley: *Organization Development and Change* (West, 1997).
- Daum, Juergen H.: *Intangible Assets and Value Creation* (Wiley, 2003).
- Gharajedaghi, Jamshid: *Systems Thinking: Managing Chaos and Complexity* (Butterworth Heinemann, 1999).
- Haeckel, Stephan H.: *Adaptive Enterprise: Creating and Leading Sense and Respond Organizations* (Harvard Business School, 1999).
- Handy, Charles B.: *Understanding Organisations* (Penguin Books, 1993).
- Henderson, Bruce A. and Jorge L. Larco: *Lean Transformation* (Oaklea Press, 2002).
- Hofstede, Geert: *Cultures and Organisations: Software of the Mind – Intercultural Cooperation and Its Importance for Survival* (McGraw Hill, 1996).
- Holweg, Matthias and Frits K. Pil: *The Second Century: Reconnecting Customer and Value Chain through Build-to-Order* (MIT Press, 2004).

- Jackson, Michael C.: *Systems Approaches to Management* (Kluwer Academic/Plenum Publisher, 2000).
- Jonker, Jan: *Toolbook For Organizational Change: A Practical Approach for Managers* (Van Gorcum, 1995).
- Kotter, John P.: *Leading Change* (Harvard Business School, 1996).
- Mintzburg, Henry: *The Rise and Fall of Strategic Planning* (Prentice Hall, 1985).
- Lusk-Brook, Kathleen, John Bray and George Litwin: *Mobilizing the Organisation: Bringing Strategy to Life* (Prentice Hall, 1995).
- Murman, Earll M., Tom Allen and Joel Cutcher-Gershenfeld: *Lean Enterprise Value: Insights from MIT's Lean Aerospace Initiative* (Palgrave Macmillan, 2002).
- Porter, Michael E.: *Competitive Advantage* (Free Press, 1985).
- Porter, Michael E.: *Competitive Strategy: Techniques for Analyzing Industries and Competitors* (Simon & Schuster, 1998).
- Scott, Mark C.: *Reinspiring the Corporation* (Wiley, 2000).
- Shinkle, George and Mike Smith: *Transforming Strategy into Success: How to Implement a Lean Management System* (Productive Publications, 2004).

Other

- Calvert, Natalie (ed.): *Gower Handbook of Call and Contact Centre Management* (Gower, 2004).
- Camrass, Roger and Martin Francombe: *Atomic: Reforming the Business Landscape into the New Structures of Tomorrow* (Capstone, 2003).
- Einstein Network: *The Business Channel* (Programme 1290, 2004).
- Goodwin, Brian: 'All for one ... one for all', in *New Scientist*, vol. 2138 (June 1998).
- Jones, Daniel T. and James P. Womack: 'Lean Consumption', in *Harvard Business Review* (March 2005).
- Lacey, Robert: *Ford* (Heinemann, 1986).
- Landmark Education: www.landmarkforum.com (workshops on personal change).
- Marr, Bernard: *Performance Measurement and Management: Public and Private Sector* (Cranfield School of Management, July 2004).
- Marr, B. and A. Neely: *Managing and Measuring for Value: the Case of Call Centre Performance* (Cranfield School of Management, July 2004).
- Morita, Akio: *Made in Japan: Akio Morita and Sony* (Collins, 1987).

- Rupert, Mark: *Producing Hegemony: The Politics of Mass Production and American Global Power* (Cambridge University Press, 1995).
- Taylor, P. and P. Bain: 'An assembly line in the head: work and employee relations in the call centre', in *Industrial Relations Journal* 30:2 (1999).
- Tseng, Mitchell M. and Frank T. Piller: *The Customer Centric Enterprise: Advances in Mass Customization and Personalization* (Springer, 2003).
- Zilstra, Fred (ed.): *European Journal of Work and Organizational Psychology – Call Centre Work: Smile By Wire* (Psychology Press, 2002).